THE MONTESSORI MANUAL

OF

CULTURAL SUBJECTS

THE MONTESSORI MANUAL
OF
CULTURAL SUBJECTS

A Guide for Teachers

by

MARJORIE B. KOCHER

Publishers

T. S. DENISON & COMPANY, INC.

Minneapolis

T. S. DENISON & COMPANY, INC.

Standard Book Number: 513-01262-1
Library of Congress Card Number: 72-189243
Printed in the United States of America
by The Brings Press
Copyright © MCMLXXIII by T. S. Denison & Co., Inc.
Minneapolis, Minn. 55437

Contents

Preface

The significance of Maria Montessori's teachings is even greater today than over fifty years ago. Dr. Montessori stressed the right of the child to know and to participate in the world around him. She envisioned vast possibilities for a peaceful and harmonious society based on the characteristics of the normalized child. Man himself would be the ultimate value in a civilization based on the child and his values rather than on the adult and adult values. Dr. Montessori impresses upon us that the important work of the child is to construct the man he is to become. She has shown the conditions necessary for the child to develop into a higher type of personality —more mentally alert, capable of concentration, more socially adaptable, more independent and at the same time more disciplined and obedient.[1] What better foundations are possible for the development of the child into an integrated adult, equipped to meet the pressures of today and solve the problems of tomorrow?

Pressures bear down upon us from every side. Civilization is threatened by a multitude of problems such as overpopulation, the destruction of our environment from pollution of the air we breathe and the water we drink and the ever-present possibility of destruction by a nuclear holocaust. We are told that in ten to twenty years the peoples of the earth will all be wearing gas masks in order to survive in the poisonous atmosphere brought about by modern technology. The effect on unborn generations is not yet known. That same technology can land man on the moon and return him safely to earth, but so far it has failed to solve the problems necessary for human survival on earth.

Society is in a state of upheaval. Signs of turmoil and unrest are all around us. Wars, violence, increasing crime rates, riots, demonstrations and militancy are a daily part of the world our children grow up in. Scientific technology has created such far reaching changes that the very foundations of our society are threatened. Discoveries of modern technology stagger the imagination and challenge old values and beliefs. We once thought that life could only be created by God. It has now been created in a test tube. The discovery of DNA and unraveling the genetic code places man in the position of possibly controlling life itself. Information can be programmed directly into the human brain; even the blind can see by means of electronic impulse. To seek relief from the tensions of a new reality brought about by rapid technological change people turn to narcotics, new and exotic religions, or resort to an increasing reliance on authoritarianism.

Society is caught in a state of crisis and is in need of a new cultural synthesis to accommodate our modern age. The laws of

[1]E. Mortimer Standing, *Maria Montessori, Her Life and Work* (New York: Mentor-Omega, New American Library, 1962), pp. 369-70.

nature and the basis for our ethical actions are in question. Science now applies cosmic laws to change nature and truth is no longer viewed as the operation of natural laws. The Montessori movement brings special strengths to the search for a cultural synthesis.[2]

If there is hope for mankind tomorrow it lies with the child of today. He is the scientist, educator, spaceman and technician of tomorrow. How can we best equip him to cope with his environment and meet the challenges of the world into which he has come? The far-reaching concepts and ideals of Maria Montessori, based on a firm belief in the total development of the child, extend hope for the future.

I want to express my sincere appreciation to my husband, John W. Kocher for his help with the illustrations; Dorothy Lanier and Alice Sachse for reviewing the text for accuracy; and to the Board of Directors of the Eugene Montessori School, Eugene, Oregon for allowing me to photograph their equipment.

Marjorie B. Kocher

Eugene, Oregon
January 1972

[2]Richard Salzmann, "Montessori and the Revolution in Values," keynote address, Montessori Centennial Celebration, Washington, D. C., March 30, 1970.

Introduction

The term Montessori method generally brings to mind the famous apparatus for sense education and those designed for teaching basic arithmetic. There has been much discussion and writing about these. Not so familiar, however, is the application of her method of teaching cultural material to the three- to six-year-old child. Dr. Montessori believed strongly in the necessity for including the fundamentals of geography, botany, zoology, science, history, art and music in the curriculum for the very young child. Teachers are hard-pressed to find specific information on how these subjects can be presented to nursery school and kindergarten age children and what materials to use. It is my purpose to set forth a practical guide to the application of Montessori principles to the presentation of cultural materials in the early childhood classroom.

The material has been largely gathered from lecture notes, practical work sessions and class observations during a year of intensive training at the Maria Montessori Training Organization in London, England. It includes detailed instructions on the Montessori approach to the cultural subjects as presented at the Training Center and in use in many Montessori schools. No presumption is made that the exercises outlined here are the only ones intended by Dr. Montessori in presenting cultural material. They are representative of those used in the Montessori method of education.

Dr. Montessori herself made no claim that her plan was complete. Of more importance than the details of her plan is the general aim of helping the whole child to develop. The problem of presenting a cosmic curriculum can only be solved through continued experimentation and imagination. One great value of the Montessori system lies in the creative insights she used to formulate an expandable theory of education. Dr. Montessori was committed to scientific investigation and experimentation and those who would adhere to a sterile interpretation of her discoveries are lost from the very principles Montessori would have them follow. No educational method can survive without growth and the teacher must be on the lookout for new ways to apply the basic Montessori principles to the changing world about her.

During my studies at the training center I was repeatedly impressed with the logical and systematic manner in which cultural subject material was made available to the child. My previous experiences in a traditional nursery school setting had left such undertakings largely to chance and the intuition of the teacher. Equally impressive was the spontaneous and eager manner in which the children went about their learning. I particularly recall one small boy who became so fascinated at the discovery of different shapes of leaves that at the age of four he could not only recognize and name each basic shape but had also outlined them on his paper. Not yet satisfied he proceeded to get the directress to help him label each with its proper name! Had information not been freely available to this child at the right time, the moment for such learning would have been lost forever.

Before describing the classroom materials and how to introduce the cultural subjects to young children, we must examine the child's need for learning about cultural matter and briefly review the basic principles of Dr. Montessori's theory of education. It is only within that context that we can derive the full meaning of the materials and their place in the early childhood school environment.

PART I
MONTESSORI THEORY

Approach to Education

The core of the Montessori system of training children is based upon three fundamental truths regarding the nature of children:

1. Children are all different from each other and need for their fullest development the greatest possible liberty for their individualities to grow.

2. Children must learn for themselves in order to grow. The impulse to learn must come from within.

3. Under proper conditions children enjoy educating themselves more than anything else.[3]

While these facts are not so startling today as they were when Dr. Montessori first spoke of them, the remarkable difference between Dr. Montessori and other educators is the logical way she applies these principles to fit her system of education to the child. The old system of class lessons given by the teacher could not possibly meet the individual needs of more than one child at best. Dr. Montessori was quick to see that the classroom must be so organized and arranged that each child can and does teach himself. It is not necessary to impose education on the child. If he is

given a learning environment where he will be free to act and develop himself along the lines of his own inner direction, he will teach himself spontaneously.

Periods of Development

The life of man is a continuum from birth to death. Man begins as a completely dependent human being and must devote his energies to the task of growing into an independent adult. This growth from childhood to maturity seems to occur in three distinct stages of development, each accompanied by its own particular needs. The type of adult one becomes is primarily dependent upon one's early childhood experiences. The three periods of development are from:

1. birth to six years,
2. six to twelve years,
3. twelve to eighteen years.

The first period is one of tremendous change and creativity. It may be divided into two sub-phases 0 to 3 years and 3 to 6 years. Not only man's intelligence but also his psychic powers are being developed. Innumerable concepts and pieces of information are being absorbed and assimilated. The primary instruments for gathering this knowledge are the senses. The child's mind works rapidly and he absorbs his environment without consciously will-

[3]Dorothy C. Fisher, *The Montessori Manual for Teachers and Parents* (Cambridge, Mass.: Robert Bentley, Inc., 1966), p. 21.

ing it. His mind is not susceptible to direct adult influence. It is this type of mentality which is called the *absorbent mind* by Dr. Montessori.

During the three- to six-year-old phase the child continues to absorb and explore his environment but gradually develops a conscious will to act and learn. Now he takes in the world consciously through voluntary movement and use of his hands. He thereby stimulates his intellect, enriches his experience and develops himself at the same time. He retains his absorbent mind which enables him to learn spontaneously and without fatigue.

The second period of development, from six to twelve years, is one of uniform growth. It has sometimes been called the *age of instruction,* as the child is capable of learning such a fantastic amount. Everything and everyone is subject to close scrutiny. The child gradually turns from a sensory exploration of his ever-widening environment to one of abstraction.

The third period of development, like the first, is marked by great physical and mental transformation. The need to develop self-confidence is strong and the young person feels he should be treated with the dignity of an adult. The guiding purpose of this period is to find one's place as an individual in society. Dr. Montessori puts forward various suggestions on what we can do to further the child's development from six years onward. Junior and senior Montessori schools are in existence abroad but any discussion of what is being done in the later stages of development is beyond our purpose.

The Sensitive Periods

The term *sensitive period* is used by Montessori to refer to the periods of special sensibility or predispositions to be found in children in the process of development. The Dutch scientist, Hugo de Vries,

discovered sensitive periods in animal life, but Dr. Montessori was the first to discover such sensitive periods in children and make scientific use of them in education. The sensitive periods are transitory in nature and confined to the acquisition of a specific characteristic. Once evolved, the characteristic continues building to perfection, while the corresponding sensibility gradually disappears.

During each period of development the child has the sensitive periods necessary to create the abilities he needs in life. These periods come when they can have the greatest impact and go when they have served their purpose.

The child has a special sensitivity toward language development from birth to six years of age. This begins with his sensitivity to the sounds of the human voice. His desire to emulate it leads to babbling by the time he is six months. If we watch a baby we see that he will be quite still and listen intently to the sound of his mother's voice. By the age of two, most children seem to explode into language. It is as if all of a sudden they had learned the language. It is a gradual, effortless process in which the child seems guided by an inner light to sort out the speech sounds from his environment and then create his own speech. From two to six years the sensitive period for language still exists and the child continues building and perfecting his language. Part of this special interest or sensitivity is directed toward the acquisition of the basic skill of reading.

A classic example of a sensitive period from the field of biology was described by Hugo de Vries. The young caterpillar must feed on tender leaves, yet the butterfly lays its eggs near the trunk of a tree. When first developed, the caterpillar naturally wriggles toward the lightest area and there it finds its food. After the caterpillar is full grown, it can eat other food and gradually loses its sensibility to light. He no longer has any use for that particular sensitivity.[4]

Montessori observed that the child also has certain irresistible urges to particular activities at certain times. Only when the child's needs and urges toward development are satisfied as they arise can the child become fully developed. What is helpful in one period may be ineffective or harmful during the next. Hence the importance of the environment. She observed many sensitive periods during the first stage of development. Among these are sensitive periods for:

Language	0 to 6 years
Order	2 to 4 years
Interest in small objects	2½ to 6 years
Social behavior	2½ to 7 years
Training of senses	3 to 6 years
Cultural subjects	3 to 6 years

Montessori's contribution to education is perhaps most valuable in its original application of the knowledge of these periods. When the education of children is organized in relation to their sensitive periods, they work eagerly and can make enormous progress, if free to choose their own activity. The essence of a sensitive period is a burning "intellectual love," according to Dr. Montessori. Because they are transitory we should be able to recognize them as they arise, then children can learn far more at an earlier age than most people believe possible.

Learning, Indirect Preparation
and the Three Period Lesson

The concept of indirect preparation is closely associated with the processes of observing, seeing and learning. It is only possible to learn and observe what you already

have within you. This is because every impression we receive—every experience we have—leaves a trace in our subconscious mind. At a later stage reassociation takes place and the individual ties together the separate parts he learned earlier into a meaningful whole.

The best way of learning is by preparing in one stage for the skills which will be necessary in the next stage. For example, in order to play baseball one must previously have learned how to hold the ball, throw it, keep one's eye on the ball, catch it, return it, hit it, et cetera. All these skills were learned earlier by the child separately and not for the express purpose of learning to play baseball. When it comes time to learn to play baseball, however, the child is already equipped with the basic skills. He merely has to go through a process of reassociation — calling these skills to his conscious mind and using them all together to play the game of baseball. His earlier learning was, therefore, an *indirect preparation* to learning how to play the game of baseball.

In order to teach, the teacher must know the component parts of the knowledge she is trying to impart. Then she will be able to present the material in such a manner as to prepare the child in one stage for what he needs in the next. An example from the sensorial equipment is found in the cylinder blocks. By holding the pegs with the first three fingers, the child is preparing indirectly to hold a pencil and for the more advanced skill of writing. Another example is from the cultural material. The knobs on the puzzle maps of the continents are located to indicate the capital cities, an indirect preparation for later study of political geography. The idea of indirect preparation is fundamental to the whole theory of the Montessori method of education. It has analyzed each ability the child

---

[4]Maria Montessori, *The Secret of Childhood* (Bombay, India: Orient Longmans, 1936), pp. 34-38.

needs into its component parts and presented them in an attractive manner to the child. He can then experience and absorb into his subconscious the skills and impressions necessary to prepare him for later life.

The three-period lesson originated by Seguin in working with retarded children was adapted and refined by Dr. Montessori. It makes use of the three stages of learning and can be used effectively with all children to teach a variety of concepts. As an example, let us see how the three-period lesson might be used with a child who has learned to take apart and replace the pieces of the world map. In the first period the teacher shows the child two puzzle pieces. Perhaps she would arouse his interest in a friendly manner by saying, "Let's do something a little different with the puzzle today." She selects two of the pieces and isolates them from the rest of the puzzle. "This is North America," she says, as she presents that piece to the child. "North America," she says. "This is North America," the child repeats, as he handles the piece of the puzzle. This procedure is followed several times until the child makes the association between the name and the shape of North America.

The same procedure is followed with any other continent, Africa, for example. The teacher pronounces the name of the continent slowly, "This is Africa." The child repeats "Africa" and identifies the piece until the association is clear.

The second period provides opportunity for practice and repetition with the material. The teacher says "Give me Africa. Where is North America? Which is Africa?" The child responds with the appropriate action. The teacher uses this period to discover how well the child has learned but does not correct him if he makes a mistake. If he does, she will know to return to the first period of the lesson. The second stage

continues over a long period of time during which the child also works independently with the puzzle or perhaps with other children.

The third period of the lesson is introduced after the child appears to have mastered the first two stages. The child is given the opportunity to reassociate what he has learned and perfect his knowledge. The teacher hands the child a piece of the puzzle and says, "What is this?" The child responds with the correct name. "Which one is this?" the teacher might ask. If the child repeatedly responds with the correct answer, the third period of the lesson is over. New continents may be introduced the next day. The teacher reviews the old material before presenting anything new.

The Prepared Environment

Realizing the importance of the first period of development in the education of the child, Doctor Montessori stressed the need for a prepared environment. Taking into account the way in which the child absorbs knowledge during his first six years, she has prepared a special environment for him and then placed the child within it and given him the freedom to move, work and develop, absorbing what he finds there.

It is necessary to have a prepared environment for the child as the usual home is made for the lives of adults—not children. The more complex civilization in which the adult lives, the more it becomes necessary to provide a particularly prepared environment for the child.

The first aim of the prepared environment is to help the child grow to be independent. For total child development the environment must contain elements which will satisfy his basic needs and tendencies. Activities presented must be designed to help the child adapt to his own particular existence. The environment should be constructed in proportion to the child's physical needs. This means not only that the furnishings but also the windows, stairs, toilets and other parts of the building itself should be child-size. This idea is so widely-accepted today, credit is not always given to Montessori for originating it. In order to bring in helpful experiences and exclude those which are harmful, the environment should be physically attractive, having food, light, air, and opportunity for free movement. It should also supply those factors which will satisfy the child's intellectual, moral and social needs and religious instincts.

The activities themselves should be attractive to the child, interesting and present a challenge. There must be a built-in control of error in the materials to stimulate repeated exploration and eventual perfection. This facilitates the process of self-teaching and growth of independence. The experiences provided should be representative of the outside world and presented in a systematic way. Our aim is to help the child recognize ordered principles in his environment.

Above all, the environment itself should be *orderly*. "A place for everything—and everything in its place" is the first law in a Montessori classroom. It should also be emphasized that without a trained directress to act as a dynamic link between the child and the prepared environment, the environment itself would be useless. The directress is an essential part of the environment and is responsible for keeping it in order and in good repair. She introduces the child to the activity, then lets him grow through using it, observing his progress and guiding him when necessary.

The directress must be an astute observer, knowing how and when to give any particular lesson to a particular child or group. Her goal is to promote the child's

independence, free choice and spontaneous activity. Her ideal is that the child should increasingly become the more active partner in the environment and herself the more passive.

To assist the child along the path toward independence the directress must develop the art of serving the spirit of the child—not his body. He must become physically independent and self-sufficient and so must learn to care for his own bodily needs. To become independent he needs to use his own free choice. He has to become capable of independent thought by working alone without interruption. The knowledge of the directress that the child's development follows a path of successive stages of development must guide her behavior toward the child. To serve the child at this level of love is to feel one is serving the spirit of man and setting it on its path to freedom.

Cultural Material in the Classroom

In the broadest sense the study of cultural subjects includes the fields of mathematics, reading, writing and language development. Since literature on the Montessori method of teaching these subjects is readily obtainable, the cultural subjects here are taken to mean such things as geography, botany, zoology, science, art, history and music. Why is it important that the young child learn about these things? To understand the reasons for including this material in our prepared environment, we must consider the goals of our education and what the child's needs are for development.

Our goal is to assist the child to develop his own personality, adapted to his particular time and place with a view toward functioning independently as a cooperative member of society. We try to provide possibilities for the child to develop fully in body, mind and spirit. So we must help the child learn to cope with life, face reality and live according to the basic laws of life. In other words, we must help him *adapt*.)

It is important to include the cultural subjects in our prepared environment if we are to help the child adapt to life, as they are part of the world around him. Man cannot exist without them. Our world contains language and mathematics and also the world of flowers, plants, animals, music, geography, history and art. In order to adapt, the individual must know something about all of these things. We must give the child at each period of development the keys to understanding that will reinforce his explorations in all areas of life. This is done gradually and by isolating a particular quality in order to give the child's mind a point of focus.

In order to adapt to life, both the world of natural phenomena and the man-made world, knowledge is needed. To acquire knowledge the child needs the freedom to explore and to have the opportunity to exercise his natural curiosity. Our aim is to provide him with an environment containing keys to all areas of understanding which he is then free to explore. Dr. Montessori recognized that it is not possible to give formalized lessons on cultural subjects to a very young child. His mind is not yet capable of learning in this manner. The Montessori approach is to provide him with sensorial keys that will open up new worlds for him when he is ready. Each area of exploration contains further keys suited to the child's progressing stages of development which in turn open up other worlds to explore.

What are the characteristics of the young explorer? What are his needs during the period of development from three to six years? This is the motor-sensory period of development. It is characterized by what Montessori calls the absorbent mind, during which the child is primarily concerned with mentally constructing his own personality. He is intensely interested in everything around him, even the tiniest object. He needs activities that satisfy his need for movement and sensorial exploration. He also needs activities which will help to develop his physical independence and sensitivity to language and bring about order into his world. He has a special sensitivity to words and works diligently to enrich his vocabulary. For his own safety and security it is necessary for his explorations to take place in a limited environment which allows him freedom to choose what he is to learn. Then, as Dr. Montessori says, "Let the child discover for himself."

Exercises of Practical Life

The material we provide as keys to the environment must give the child opportunity to learn by working with it. For each area of activity, appropriate Practical Life Exercises must be provided. The term *practical life* is used by Dr. Montessori to describe those routines having to do with the care of the child's own person and the care of the environment. These provide a means of motor education and help to answer the needs of the sensitive period through which he is passing. The child is shown precisely how to perform each exercise, then is free to practice as often as he wishes. Such functions are routine to us but are new and exciting to a young child. He needs to be shown how to do them.

The term *synthetic movement* was used by Montessori to describe such ordered movements directed by the mind to an intelligible purpose as are necessary to complete these tasks. The child does them from a compelling inner urge, as they help to satisfy his basic tendencies such as the needs for order, repetition and perfection, exploration and movement. The satisfaction of such basic tendencies in turn promotes a sense of security in the child which contributes to his whole personality—physical, mental and spiritual.

Examples of practical life exercises in relation to the cultural subjects would be wiping up spilled paint, washing the table, cleaning paint brushes, sweeping up bits of paper, watering plants and flowers, cleaning pet cages and so on. The list is unending and depends on the particular classroom activity.

Sensorial Keys

Geography may be introduced at the sensorial level through land and water forms. At first it is an exercise of pouring water into the land and water forms. Later the child can learn the language associated with the different formations by means of classified geography cards. These can be used first at the prereading stage and later at the reading stage. The cards in turn provide keys to the study of maps. First he has the globe showing the main land and water formations, then the continents. Later, he learns to take apart a puzzle map of the continents. When he can readily take out the pieces and replace them, you teach him the names. He proceeds to a puzzle map of his own continent and its countries. When he knows how to take this apart and replace the pieces, again he can learn the names of the countries and later the names of the capitals. Finally, he will want to consolidate his knowledge and make his own maps.

Geography can also be introduced through the practical life exercise of walking on the line. This is an exercise in movement leading to balance and control. A line is either drawn or painted on the floor in the shape of an ellipse. The teacher then shows the child how to walk by placing the heel and toe both on the line. The child is given a flag to carry and for a long time works at walking and carrying. Then one day he'll show an interest in what kind of a flag it is, or he'll want to make his own flag to carry. Following this activity, he will then need to be given the proper name of the flag to express his experience. This in turn leads to a study of other flags and political geography. Each key unlocks a doorway to another world which the child explores for as long as he wishes. There he discovers new keys which further his explorations and in turn open up new doorways to even larger worlds about him.

In short the essentials of the presentation of cultural subjects to a young child are as follows:

1. A prepared environment with details that excite interest in cultural subjects such as plants, flowers, pets and maps.

2. Related exercises of practical life to extend interest.

3. Sensorial keys and materials for activity still further extending knowledge.

4. Language to express his knowledge.

5. Related handwork such as clay modeling, painting.

If we keep in mind that the child's development, constructing his own personality, adapting to the world about him, are the goals we are trying to achieve, we will seize all possible opportunities. There is no question about expecting the child to master the cultural subjects. What is needed is a special method whereby all the basic factors of culture can be introduced. At this age the cultural items will be received as seeds which will later germinate into real culture. If you were to ask her how many such seeds should be sown, Montessori would answer, "As many as possible."[5]

---

[5]Standing. p. 364.

Photo at right: Exercise in practical life. Watering the plants.

—Photo taken at Montessori International School, Cottage Grove, Oregon

Photo below: Puzzle map of the United States.

—Photo taken at Montessori International School, Cottage Grove, Oregon

PART II
PRESENTATION OF CULTURAL SUBJECTS

Geography
PRACTICAL LIFE EXERCISES
Pouring with Geography Models

Fig. 1 — Pouring Water With Geography Models
—Photo taken at Eugene Montessori School

MATERIAL

Eight rectangular baking pans containing models of the land and water forms made of plasticine or other waterproof modeling material. In addition, a small pitcher of water, and a tiny boat made from a nutshell. (See section on art.) Formations represented are island, lake, cape, bay, peninsula, gulf, isthmus and strait.

PRESENTATION

Select two corresponding land and water formations, e.g., a lake and an island. Show the child exactly how to pour water so that the island rises out and only a small portion covers the base. Similarly, the lake should not overflow the surrounding land. Ask the child if he wishes to try. The rest of the forms may follow.

EXERCISE 1

As presented.

EXERCISE 2

Give the child a boat made from a nutshell. The child pours the water into the models and discovers where the boat can sail.

AGE

3 years onwards.

INDIRECT AIM

An introduction to physical geography.

DIRECT AIM

Coordination of movement.

CONTROL OF ERROR

The amount of water must be correct.

LANGUAGE

The names of the landforms can be taught whenever the child asks for them. This can be done by the three-period lesson and later in connection with the geography cards.

OUTDOOR EXERCISE

After a rain, take the children outside to discover how many lakes, islands, gulfs, bays, capes and peninsulas they can find in the garden.

Flags for Walking the Line

MATERIAL

A set of flags of all nations of a suitable size for carrying. These are displayed on a stand.

Fig. 2 — Walking on the Line With Flags
—Photo taken at Eugene Montessori School

PRESENTATION

After the child has learned to do walking on the line without carrying anything, he may select a flag from the stand and carry it around. Later, he carries two flags —one in each hand.

EXERCISE 1

As in presentation.

EXERCISE 2

The child may color or paint his own flags, drawing them on paper.

LANGUAGE

The names of the countries represented by the flags. Teach by the three-period lessons, when the child shows an interest. Begin with the child's own flag.

AGE

3 years onwards.

AIM

Coordinated movement.

INDIRECT AIM

Introduction to political geography.

SENSORIAL KEYS

Globe Showing Land and Water

MATERIAL

A small globe having a rough, sandpaper texture representing the earth. The water areas are smooth and painted blue. The sandpaper areas may be pasted by the teacher onto a small globe or one can be purchased already made.

PRESENTATION

The globe is kept in an easily accessible place. Explore the globe during a group lesson to see which areas are land and which are water. See how much of each can be found.

PARALLEL MATERIALS

Events chart and puzzle maps are in use. The geography models are on a low table available for the child to pour in the waters of the world.

Globe Showing Continents of the World

A second, small globe shows the continents in color. It is important to have a

A—Continents   B—Land and Water
Fig. 3 — Globes   —Photo taken at Eugene Montessori School

large, detailed globe and maps in the room for further exploration and comparison.

AGE

3 years onwards.

DIRECT AIM

To help the child become aware of the world he lives in. To give a tactile impression of the land and water forms. To arouse and stimulate interest leading to deeper study later.

INDIRECT AIM

A first step toward study of physical and political geography.

Puzzle Map of the World

MATERIAL

A large, colorful wooden world map. The continents may be removed and replaced by knobs.

PRESENTATION

The directress and the child take out the pieces and mix them up. Show the child with each piece how to work the puzzle. Try the piece one direction and then another, finally arriving at the correct place. Allow the child to work the puzzle alone when he is ready.

CONTROL

The control of error is built into the material.

AGE

3 years onwards.

LANGUAGE

The names of the continents taught by the three-period lesson.

FOLLOW-UP MATERIAL

Puzzle-map of North America or child's own continent.

Puzzle-map of United States or child's own country.

Puzzle-map of California or child's own province.

Puzzle-maps of other continents.

25

Fig. 4 — Puzzle Maps
—Photo taken at Eugene Montessori School

DIRECT AIM

To provide a sensorial key to the land masses of the world, then to his own continent and country.

INDIRECT AIM

The knobs of the separate puzzle pieces are the locations of the capital cities.

Preparation for study of political geography.

HANDWORK

1. The child can trace the outline of the pieces and construct his own maps.

2. Provide the child with his own outline map and have him fill in the colors on the continents, adding flags.

3. The child can make clay models of the separate countries.

ASSOCIATED ACTIVITIES

Have a well-equipped library for further exploration.

Dolls from other lands.

Community resources — may include parents or others willing to show slides or costumes from other countries.

Read stories.

Construct houses of cardboard. Make and color cutouts of people to go with each kind of house. Use these in conjunction with the maps.

Collect pictures of other lands and mount them.

Maps with Flags

MATERIAL

Two plywood maps of Europe painted yellow for the land and blue for the waters. On the first map the countries are drawn and represented by their flags.

The second map is similar, but the countries are not named and have a tiny hole to indicate where the flag should be placed. A small box accompanies this map and contains the flags of the countries. A map of the United States and state flags may be used in a similar manner.

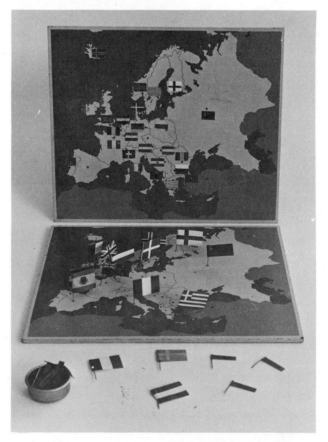

Fig. 5 — Maps of Europe With Flags
—Photo taken at Eugene Montessori School

PRESENTATION

Place both maps on the child's table. Show the child that the separate flags can be matched to the ones on the map. Then pin the separate flag onto the second map. After you demonstrate how to match two or three flags and pin them onto the map, let the child continue, if he seems ready.

CONTROL

The flags marked on the first map. (Refer back to these)

AGE

3½ years onwards.

DIRECT AIM

To match the maps.

INDIRECT AIM

To recognize the flags of the world, especially his own continent. To make full use of the absorbent mind for later study.

LANGUAGE

The names of the countries represented by the flags can be taught by the three-period lesson.

HANDWORK

Painting flags and drawing the maps.

FOLLOW-UP EXERCISES

1. There is a similar map with names of the countries and also separate names to be matched and pinned in place.

2. Another map having the names of the capital cities of the countries of the child's continent. Separate name slips are matched as before.

3. The child may place the names of the countries, their capitals and the flags on the blank map. This will be after he is very proficient with the previous exercises.

AGE

5 to 5½ years approximately.

Fig. 6 — People of the World—Japanese   —Photo taken at Eugene Montessori School

People of the World

MATERIAL

A box containing various sets of pictures made of colored cardboard representing the peoples of the world and how they live. Houses, transportation, food, clothing, children and geography are depicted. The figures are mounted on stands and can be moved about. There is also an appropriate background for the setting.

PRESENTATION

The directress tells a group about the environment—e.g.: the desert, and sets up the figures. Books, stories, map study, song and dance all are related activities that have been going on beforehand.

EXERCISE 1

The child takes out one set and constructs it to represent the community.

EXERCISE 2

After each set is presented and learned separately, the sets may be mixed. The child can then sort the figures and find their correct backgrounds.

EXERCISE 3

Find where the people live on the puzzle maps and globe.

CONTROL OF ERROR

The directress at first, then the child's understanding.

DIRECT AIM

A first study of people of the world and how they live.

INDIRECT AIM

Indirect preparation for social sciences.

AGE

4 years and onwards.

History
PERSONAL TIME LINE

MATERIAL

A roll of graph paper six inches wide, one square to the inch, also colored pencils and a ruler. Photographs brought from home to represent each year of the child's life. Pictures from magazines may be substituted, if photographs are not available.

Fig. 7 — Time Line
—Photo taken at Eugene Montessori School

PRESENTATION

Rule off one foot of the graph paper to represent each year of the child's life. A different color is used for each year. The child can then rule off one square for each month. The date of birth and yearly intervals are recorded along with the outstanding events of each year. The child can paste appropriate pictures on the chart. He and the directress should work together, with the child doing as much of the work as possible.

AGE

5 years and onwards.

DIRECT AIM

To give the child an understanding of time and a beginning of understanding his own personal history.

INDIRECT AIM

To lay the groundwork for the Historical Time Line.

EVENTS CHART

MATERIAL

A large rectangular board painted with two contrasting colors. Enamel paint wears well for this purpose. One-half contains pictures representing past events. The other half is for pictures of current interest.

PRESENTATION

The directress introduces the board by taping up pictures and telling about them. Present only one basic idea at a time. The pictures on the top should be related to those on the bottom and be changed frequently. For example, the travels of the Presidential family can be pasted. The names of the places are then related to the maps of the world, and the globe.

AIM

A key to the understanding of time.

INDIRECT AIM

A foundation for later historical study.

AGE

3 years and onwards.

BOOKS AND STORIES

Have in your book corner a book showing the flags of all the countries in the world. Have books telling about how it is to live in other countries—festivals, food, schools, work, and customs. These books should contain illustrations showing national costumes, homes, food, kinds of work and recreation. Teach songs and dances from other lands. Know and use your community resources. Parents may have color slides, costumes, dishes or other materials

to share. Have a book of folktales and poetry from other nations in the book corner. Books of national heroes and personalities are also valuable. Here again parents may help.

Science
ELECTRICITY

Simple Circuit

MATERIAL

A chemical battery, wire, switch, bulb.

EXERCISE

Make an electric circuit by attaching the wires to the battery, the switch and the light bulb, as shown in the diagram. Turn

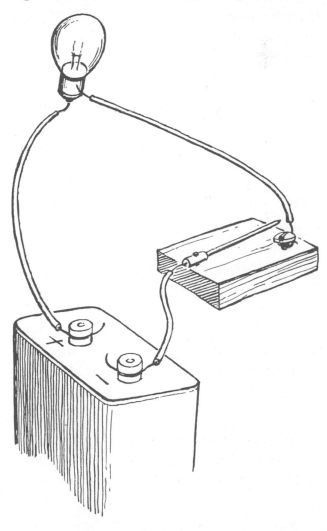

Fig. 8 — Electric Circuit and Switch

on the switch (completing the circuit) and observe the light in the bulb. Unfasten the wire (breaking the circuit), and show that the light goes out. Fasten the end of the wire to the battery again and the bulb again lights up.

AIM

To demonstrate that electricity flows in a circular direction. We cause the electricity to flow by completing the circuit.

Electrical Exploration

MATERIAL

Simple circuit and various materials from the environment—coin, pin, lead pencil, wood, plastic, cork and paper.

EXERCISE 1

Investigate various materials to see if they will conduct electricity. Place a piece of cork between the end of the wire and the battery. It does not conduct—no light. Place a piece of wood in the same position. It does not conduct. Electricity will pass through one end of a lead pencil and out the other, lighting the bulb.

EXERCISE 2

Walk around the classroom discovering which materials will conduct electricity and which will act as insulators. The child may continue the exploration. Show him the proper way to plug in appliances and turn on switches and caution him about safe practices.

AIM

To give basic experiences with electricity. To demonstrate the flow of electricity and show the conductors and insulators.

AGE

3½ years and onwards. Caution the child about dangers of electricity.

LIGHT

Exploration of Room with Lens

Fig. 9 — Exploration With Lens

Have an assortment of objects such as a leaf, seashell, a specimen of handwriting, a nail, rock and a clip in a box. The child examines each of these with a magnifying (convex) lens at his own table. Later, he may take the lens with him and explore the room.

Camera

Hold your lens upright facing a window, electric light, or a lighted candle. Hold a piece of white cardboard on the opposite side of the lens and several inches away. Move the paper backwards and forwards until you see a sharp image of the window or other light source on the card. The image will be upside down.

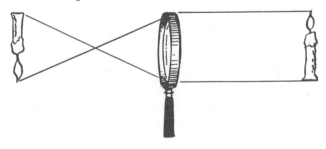

Fig. 10 — Principle of Camera Lens

AIM

To provide a basic key to the understanding of light. To demonstrate that light rays are bent by a lens.

3½ years onwards.

Shadows

MATERIAL

A piece of white cardboard, the electric circuit or a flashlight, a translucent object such as a plastic-handled screwdriver, and any solid object.

EXERCISE 1

Switch on the light. Place the screwdriver between the light and the shadowboard to throw a shadow on the board.

Move the object in relation to the light. Observe the change in dimension and clarity of the shadow.

Move the shadow-board in relation to the object and the light.

Move the light in relation to the object. Observe changes in size of shadow as above.

The child continues to explore.

AIM

To give basic experience with light. To show that light travels in a straight line. To show that light does not pass through solid objects—such as the metal part of the screwdriver. To show that some objects are translucent.

MAGNETS

Sand and Iron Filings

Obtain iron filings from a metal-work shop. Place a small amount of sand in a saucer. The teacher tells the story of the good king who was greatly loved by all his subjects. (Place teaspoonful of iron filings on the sand in a pile.) One day the subjects went into the forest. (Begin to mix filings with sand.) They went farther and farther into the forest, until the king could no longer see them. (Mix filings into sand until well blended.)

When the king called them, he was loved so dearly, that the subjects all came back to him out of the forest! (At this point,

perform some "magic." Place a magnet concealed by a handkerchief over the sand and see the subjects jump up out of the forest!)

The child is free to explore this use of the magnet.

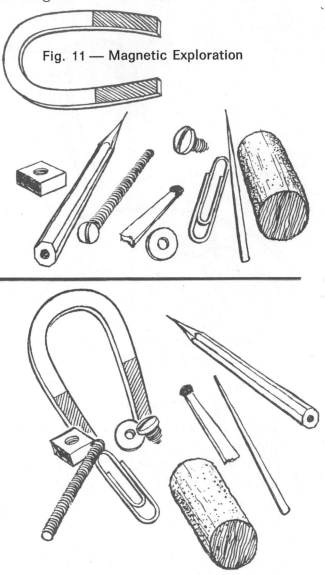

Fig. 11 — Magnetic Exploration

Sorting Prepared Objects

On the shelf the magnet is kept, have a box of assorted objects such as a key, a coin, cork, a screw, wire, rubber-band, pin, toothpick, et cetera. The child holds the magnet next to each of the materials to discover which are attracted by the magnet and which are not. He does this at his table.

Exploration of Room

The child can take the magnet with him, placing it next to the various materials he sees in the room. He tests the door, the window, the tables, the door handles, metal trays and other objects.

Compass

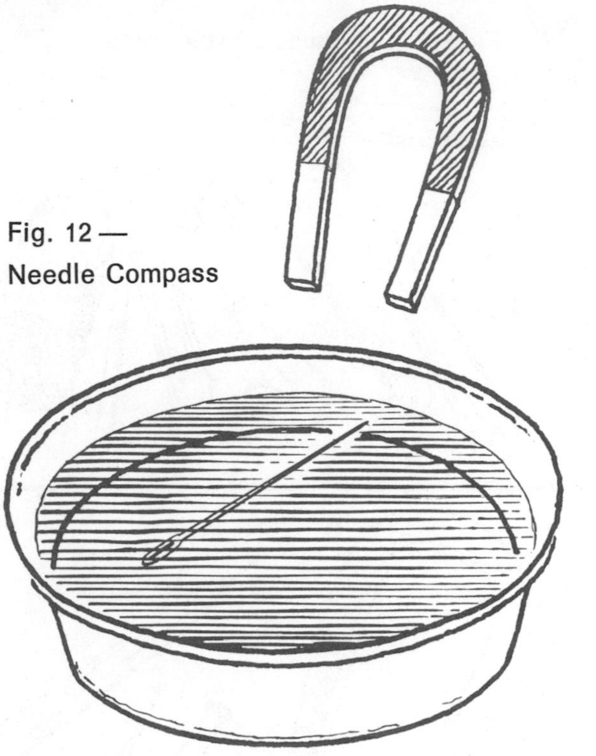

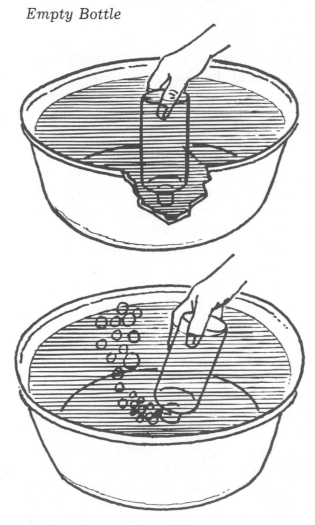

Fig. 12 —
Needle Compass

Make a simple compass by stroking a needle several times in one direction over one pole of the magnet. Fill a small vessel with water. Float the needle gently, directly on the water, or place it on a piece of paper floated on the water. The needle will turn so that it points north and south. It is attracted by earth's magnetic pole.

Hold the magnet over the needle. Move it back and forth and watch the needle move. It is now controlled by the hand magnet, which is closer.

Control of Paper Clip through Cardboard

Hold a thin piece of cardboard next to the end of the magnet. With the other hand, place a paper clip underneath the cardboard. The magnet will hold the paper clip through cardboard. Move the magnet and watch the clip move. Explore other materials—glass, wood, foil, et cetera.

AGE

3½ years onwards.

AIMS

To give basic sensorial experiences with magnetic force. To show which objects are attracted by magnetic force and which are not. To show that magnetism acts through matter.

ATMOSPHERE

Empty Bottle

Fig. 13 — Empty Bottle Really Contains Air

MATERIAL

A large vessel of water, such as a dishpan or wash basin, also a glass jar having

32

a small opening. The height of the jar must not exceed the water level in the vessel.

EXERCISE

Fill the vessel with water. Place the jar straight down into the water, upside down. The water will not go into the jar. What is keeping it from going inside the jar? Tilt the jar slowly. Observe the bubbles rising to the surface, as the air forces its way upward, allowing the water to enter the jar.

Empty Bottle with Rubber Tube

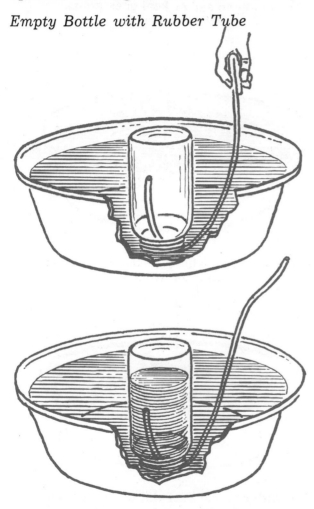

Fig. 14 — Empty Bottle With Rubber Tube

Place the empty jar upside down in the water, as quickly as possible. Pinch one end of a rubber tube and place the other end under the jar opening. Release the tube and note the water rise to the same level as the large container. What has happened?

Water replaces the air released, when we release our hold on the tube. Suck on the end of the tube to remove any remaining air. Water level again rises in the jar. Introduce air again. Blow through tube. Water level falls in jar. Bubbles rise. Repeat process.

Two Empty Bottles

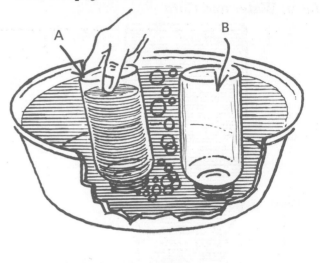

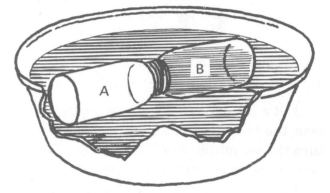

Fig. 15 — Two Empty Bottles

MATERIALS

Two glass jars of equal size and having the same size opening. A large container of water.

EXERCISE

Place the two jars simultaneously upside down in the water so that they touch the bottom of the container. As in preceding experiments, the water does not enter the jars. Slowly tilt one jar so that it fills

33

with water. Replace its mouth against the bottom of the container. Quickly raise the mouths of both jars and place firmly together. Turn the jars and note that the water leaves jar "A" and enters jar "B," showing that the air and the water have exchanged places.

Jar of Water and Card

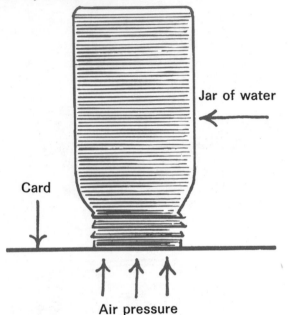

Fig. 16 — Water Held in Jar by Air Pressure

Fill a jar with water. Place a cardboard over the top of the jar. Hold it in place and turn the jar upside down. Carefully remove your hand from the card. Does the card stay in place? Why? Would this work if the glass were only half-filled? Try and see. Why does this happen?

The card only stays in place when the jar is filled with water. The pressure exerted by the atmosphere is greater than that exerted by the water.

Blowing Bubbles

Dip a straw into a container of water and blow air through it. The rising bubbles demonstrate the presence of air.

Fig. 17 — Blowing Boats

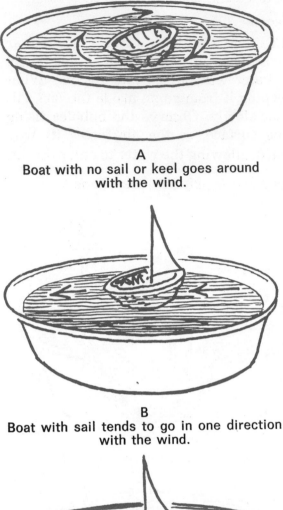

A
Boat with no sail or keel goes around with the wind.

B
Boat with sail tends to go in one direction with the wind.

C
Boat with sail and keel will go forward and backward with the wind.

Blowing the Boat

MATERIALS

Large container of water, a straw and a walnut shell boat having a sail made from a match and a piece of paper. A second boat made of a half of a walnut shell. There is also a piece of cork with a keel and a sail.

EXERCISES

1. The walnut shell boat is placed on the water. Blow the boat on the water. Blow the boat and note how it moves about.

2. Place the boat with a sail on the water and blow. This time, it tends to go in one direction, as the sail helps direct the boat in the wind.

3. Place the cork with sail and keel on the water and blow first from one direction then another. This boat will only go forward or backward (not around), as the keel acts as a stabilizer.

Bicycle Pump

Show the child how to take the pump apart and reassemble. Lubricate with Vaseline.

Press handle of pump down, feeling the air come out the end. Place finger over the opening and again press the handle. The air is now compressed, making it much more difficult to operate the pump.

Blow air into the valve. The handle moves away from the pump.

Suck and inhale through the opening. This draws the handle back to the pump.

AIM

To demonstrate the elasticity of air.

Siphoning

MATERIALS

A large vessel of water, rubber tubing and a pail.

EXERCISE

Place a pail below the water vessel. Hold one end of the tubing at the bottom of the container and shape the remaining portion to conform to the contour of the container. Leave a small section outside the container. When the water is seen coming to the end of the tube, stem the flow by pinching the tube. Place the end of the tubing into the bucket and release the pressure. The water continues to flow into the bucket until it reaches the same level

as the water in the container. Raise the bucket to demonstrate this. Lower the bucket and water flows again.

Siphoning With Two Jars

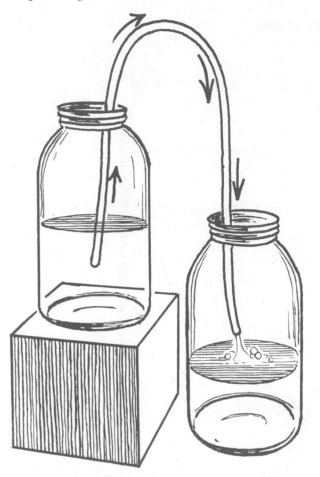

Fig. 18 — Siphoning With Two Jars

MATERIALS

The same as above except two jars are used and no bucket.

EXERCISE

Place the tube in the water container as before. Siphon water into one of the jars. When the jar is nearly filled, remove the other end of the tube from the container, while pinching it. Place this end of the tube into the second jar at a slightly lower level. Release the pressure on the tube and the water will flow from jar "A" to jar "B." This may be repeated as often as desired.

Place both jars on a level surface while the siphoning action is continuing. The action stops when the water level is the same in both jars.

Fountain

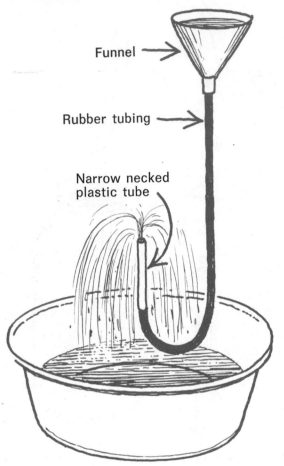

Funnel

Rubber tubing

Narrow necked plastic tube

Fig. 19 — Fountain

MATERIAL

Rubber tubing, funnel, a narrow, clear glass tube, and water.

EXERCISE

Insert the glass tubing into one end of the rubber tubing and the funnel in the other. Fill the funnel with water and hold high up in the air. Hold the glass tubing upright within a water container. The water will squirt up through the glass tubing in a fine stream, making a fountain.

Candle in Limited Air

Fig. 20 — Candle in Limited Air

MATERIAL

A pie tin, a wax candle, a jar and colored water.

EXERCISE

Stand a lighted candle firmly in the center of a pie tin with a drop of melted wax or plasticine. Pour water into the tin until it is nearly full. Place a jar over the candle. Soon you see the water begin to climb up inside the bottle. Then the candle goes out. Why does this happen? The flame went out after using up some of the oxygen in the bottle. The remaining air took up less space, allowing the outside air to push the water up into the bottle.

AIM

To make the child realize we are surrounded by air. To provide basic keys to its understanding. Air exists but cannot be seen. Air exerts pressure.

AGE

3 years onwards.

36

GRAVITY

Center of Gravity

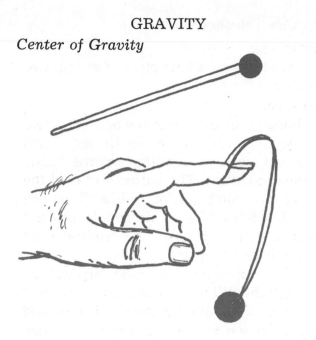

Fig. 21 — Plastic Ball Finds Center of Gravity

MATERIALS

Ball of plasticine, a piece of flexible wire.

EXERCISE

Stick the wire into the ball of plasticine. Try to balance the ball by placing the wire across the tip of your finger. When it is straight, it tends to fall.

Now, bend the wire into an arch. Place the end of the wire on the tip of your finger. Gradually adjust the size of the arch, until the ball of plasticine does not fall.

When it remains balanced, you have found the center of gravity. This demonstrates the principle of stable equilibrium.

The Pendulum

Stick a ball of plasticine or some other weight on a long piece of string. Hold the other end of the string as high as possible, or fasten it, so that the weight can swing freely. Start the pendulum. Note that each swing takes the same amount of time. A long string takes a long time. Shorten the pendulum by passing the string over a rod. The swing is now faster.

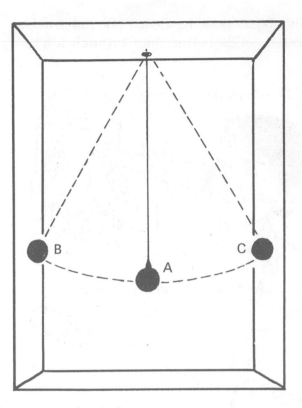

Fig. 22 — Simple Pendulum Acted Upon by Gravity

AIM

To demonstrate the basic principle of the pendulum. If its length is the same, it always takes the same time to complete one swing. If it is shortened, the swing is faster.

AGE

3½ years onwards.

SOUND

Paper Tube (or Hose-Pipe)

Place one end of a long paper tube near your mouth and speak in a soft whisper. The child listens at the other end of the tube. The sound is amplified. It travels through the air. Vibrations are compressed in the tube.

Sound through Solids

Have the child place his ear close to the end of a wooden table. Tap the opposite end of the table with your finger. Scratch the wood with your fingernail. Place a ticking watch on the opposite end of the table. What does he hear? (Sound travels through solids better than through air.)

Fig. 23 — Exploration of Sound

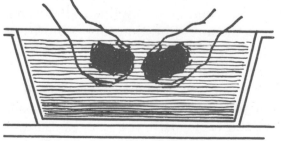

A—Sound through paper tube

B—Tin can telephone

C—Sound through solid

D—Sound through water

Tin Can Telephone

MATERIALS

Two tin cans, a long piece of string, two buttons.

EXERCISE

Punch a small hole in the bottom of two tin cans. Thread the string through each hole and tie it to a button on the inside of the can bottom. The button will hold the string so it can't pull out when the string is pulled tight. The string should be long enough so two people, one holding each can, will be far apart.

Give one can to the child. Stretch the string tight. While you talk into one can, have the child hold the other to his ear and listen. Loosen the string. Does it become harder or easier to hear? Let the child talk through the telephone to you. The sound waves of the voice travel along the tight string and are received as vibrations heard by the ear at the other end.

Sound through Liquid

Fill a container with water. Hold a rock in each hand and strike together in the air. Listen. Hold two rocks down in the water and strike them together. Listen. The sound is muffled.

AIM

To give the child basic keys to understanding the laws of sound.

AGE

3 years and onwards.

FLOATING

Sink or Float

MATERIAL

An assortment of objects of various materials for testing whether they sink or float. For example, a nutshell, leaf, feather, plasticine, marbles, rock and paper clip.

EXERCISE

The child drops one object at a time into a large vessel of water and observes whether they sink or float.

Fig. 24 — Sink or Float

Plasticine Boat

Shape a ball of plastic clay into a boat. Carefully float it on top of the water.

This shows that material which will sink in one form may float when distributed over a larger water surface.

AIM

To provide basic keys to understanding that some things float and some sink.

AGE

3 years onwards.

Botany

PREPARATION OF THE ENVIRONMENT

For the child's safety and security it is necessary to provide a prepared environment for him to explore the botanical world. Ideally, we would like a light, airy and attractive classroom with double doors opening out into a garden. The garden should be completely enclosed with a fence, so the child can wander in safety. It should contain both a cultivated area and a wild section. If there are sturdy trees, the chil-

dren should be allowed to climb them, up to a safe height.

The cultivated section should be designed with the idea that it is for the child's use and exploration. Paths should be wide enough for passage and flower beds narrow enough so a child can reach the center from either side. It is also advisable to have a concrete or asphalt play area or else a lawn with good drainage. The plants and flowers we choose for the garden should represent the various types depicted on our botanical cards and in the leaf cabinet.

Another requisite of the prepared outdoor environment is a garden shed. It should be well arranged and have a particular place for each piece of equipment. The tools and other gardening materials should be well designed and of a suitable size for children to handle. We need to have a wheelbarrow, spade, hoe, watering cans or hose and a rake. The tools and shed should be attractive and painted with a good quality outdoor paint. The children should be taught the proper handling and care of the equipment. Baskets for carrying dead leaves and soft strings for tying up plants should also be included.

The indoor environment should have a nature table to focus attention on particular aspects of plant life. The table should be low enough for the child to see what is on it. The surface should be a washable one. It should be kept simple, having no more than two or three things on it at any one time. The exhibits should be changed every few days, after the children have looked at and learned about them. The children are not yet ready for long-term experiments.

The classroom should contain well-chosen plants and flowers which will represent the basic types of leaves and flowers on our botany cards. Do not have too many varieties out at a time. They are there to arouse the child's interest and give him an opportunity to explore.

PRACTICAL LIFE EXERCISES— OUTDOOR ENVIRONMENT

Maintenance of garden shed.
How to clean the tools and replace them.
How to clean up the garden, rake leaves, stake and tie plants, cut off dead materials and dispose of them.
How to water the plants and flowers.
How to cut flowers.
How to pull up weeds from the cultivated area.

PRACTICAL LIFE EXERCISES— INDOOR ENVIRONMENT

How to water plants—some from top, some from underneath.
Remove dead flowers and leaves.
Clean the vases.
How to cut stems. (Which should be held under water, some should be cut at an angle and some straight across; when used in vases.)
Clean the saucers used as drainage dishes and for experiments.
How to dust the leaves.

SENSORIAL KEYS

The aim of the sensorial material is to provide the child with the keys to make order among the thousands of plants and flowers that exist. We give points of consciousness for exploration at a sensorial level, and do not really teach botany.

The Leaf Cabinet

There are three tray drawers in the leaf cabinet containing green wooden insets representing 14 basic leaf shapes. The background material is yellow. The insets are knobbed and may be taken out and replaced.

Fig. 25 — Leaf Cabinet and Cards
—Photo taken at Eugene Montessori School

Three sets of leaf cards accompany the leaf cabinet. Each set has the 14 leaf shapes outlined in green. The first set is a heavy outline, the next is medium and the last is narrow. The child removes the inset from the leaf cabinet, holding it with the first three fingers. With the first finger of the other hand, he gently, but firmly traces the outline of the wooden inset. Then he traces the outline on the card, and sees if he can place the inset precisely over the outline, so that none of the outline is seen. He works through all the cards and all the insets.

Basic procedure for leaf cabinet and cards is as follows:
Remove shapes and put back in place.
Encourage child to find similar shapes in the garden.
Begin your exploration in the classroom by having a variety of specimen plants to examine.
Bring leaves into the classroom and take children outside to explore. A visit

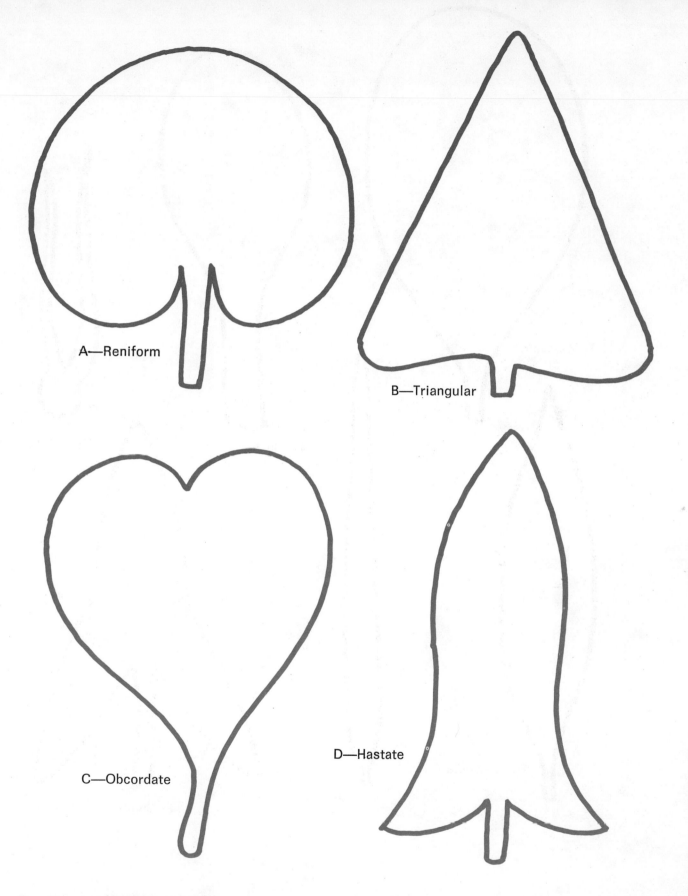

A—Reniform

B—Triangular

C—Obcordate

D—Hastate

Fig. 26 — Leaf Shapes and Language

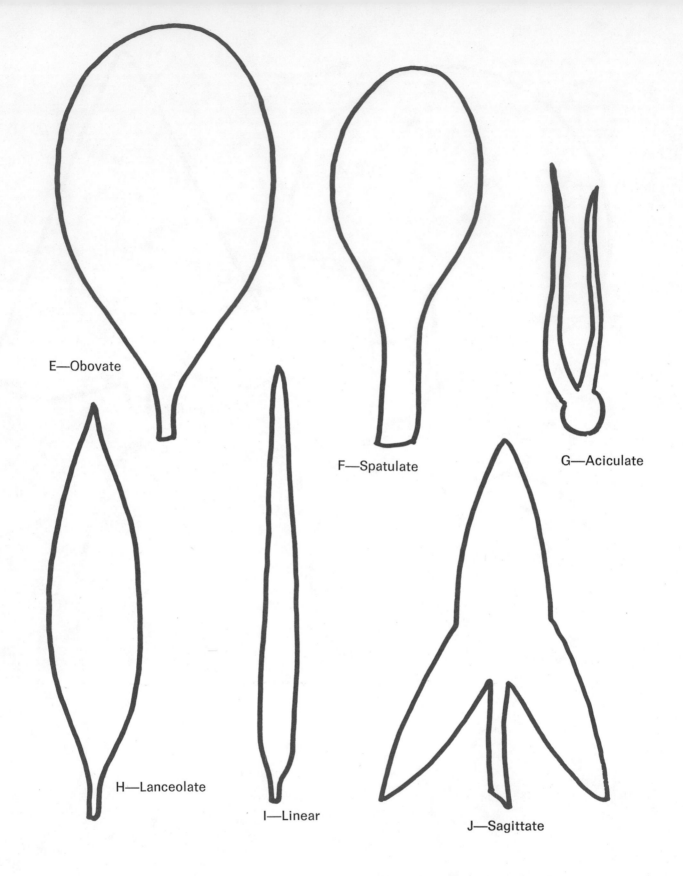

E—Obovate

F—Spatulate

G—Aciculate

H—Lanceolate

I—Linear

J—Sagittate

Fig. 26 — Leaf Shapes and Language

42

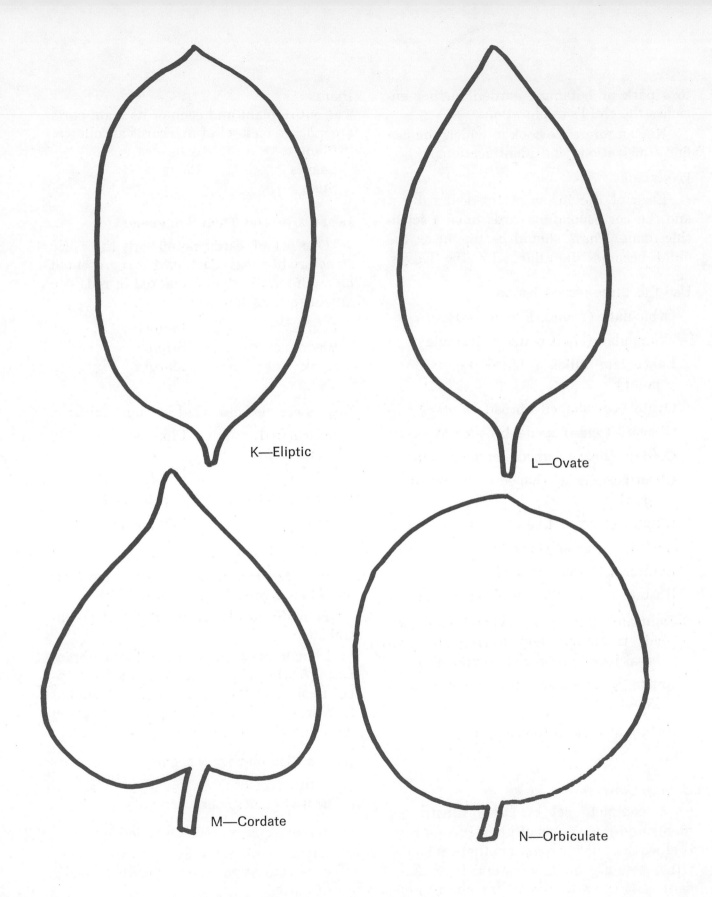

K—Eliptic

L—Ovate

M—Cordate

N—Orbiculate

Fig. 26 — Leaf Shapes and Language

to a park or botanical garden further enriches the child's explorations.

Keep a reference book in which you can find illustrations and identifications.

Each of the insets of the leaf cabinet and the corresponding cards have a scientific name. These should be taught as the child becomes familiar with the leaves.

Use the three-period lesson.

Orbiculate (round, like an orb)

Triangular (shaped like a triangle)

Lanceolate (like a lance, tapers to a point)

Ovate (egg-shaped—broad at base)

Obovate (egg-shaped—broader at apex)

Cordate (heart-shaped—broader at base)

Obcordate (heart-shaped—broader at apex)

Elliptic (shaped like an ellipse)

Spatulate (spoon-shaped)

Reniform (kidney-shaped)

Hastate (arrow-like, with flaring barbs)

Sagittate (like an arrowhead, enlongated, triangular and having the two basal lobes prolonged downward)

Linear (enlongated with nearly parallel sides)

Aciculate (a needle-like spine)

Botany Cards

A complete set of cards illustrating plants and main parts of plant-life. One set is of leaves, one for roots, another for stems. Other sets are for flowers and fruit. Each card calls the attention of the child to one particular aspect of the subject, by red markings.

Plants

The entire plant and each of its main parts are marked on a set of five cards as follows:

Plant	Axis
Leaves	Roots
Stem	

Leaf Cards and Their Language

One set of cards points out the basic structure of a leaf. Each part is represented on a different card and marked in red. The language is as follows:

Leaf	Petiole
Blade	Stipules
Apex	Margin
Veins	

Leaves are also classified by their veins:

Reticulated (matted)	Pinnate
Parallel	Palmate

Leaves are classified by their blades:

Simple	Compound

Compound Leaves

Pinnate—having a main stem and leaflets (like a rose, feather-like)

Palmate—leaflets coming out of a central stem.

Pinnate leaves may be either *parapinnate* (feather-like, equally divided on opposite sides of the stem having a terminal leaf or stem), or *imparapinnate* (having no terminal leaf or stem).

Leaves Classified by Margins

entire (smooth)
dented (not smooth, irregular)

Dented margins may be classified as:

serrate—points facing upwards
bi-serrate—two points together facing upward
crenate—curly
dentate—point looking sideways

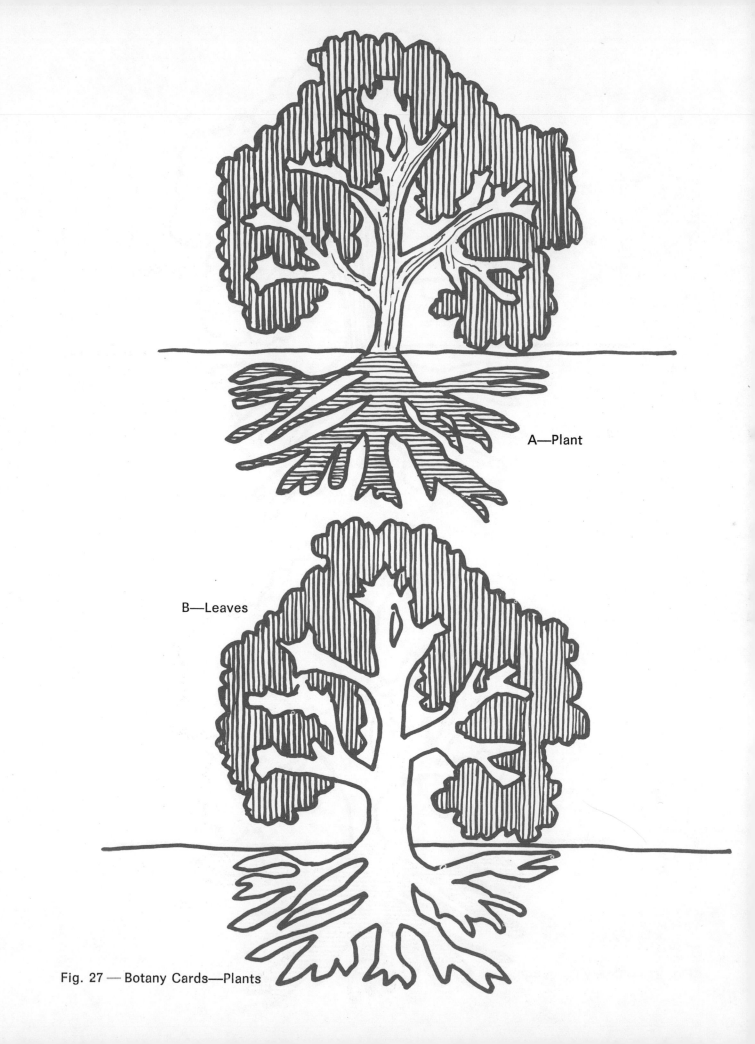

A—Plant

B—Leaves

Fig. 27 — Botany Cards—Plants

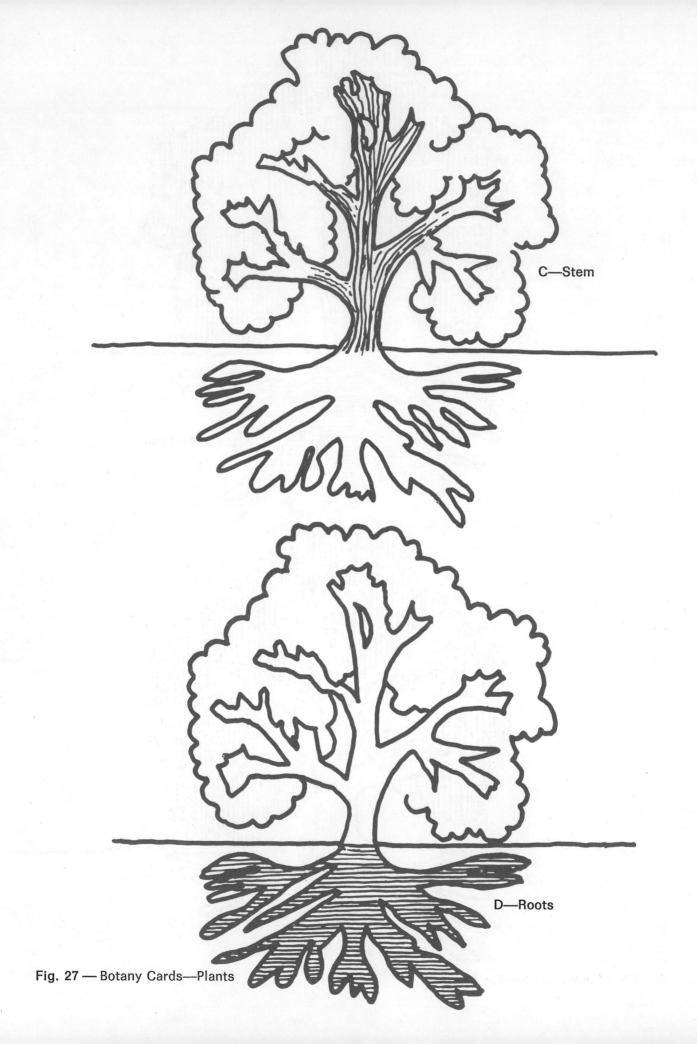

C—Stem

D—Roots

Fig. 27 — Botany Cards—Plants

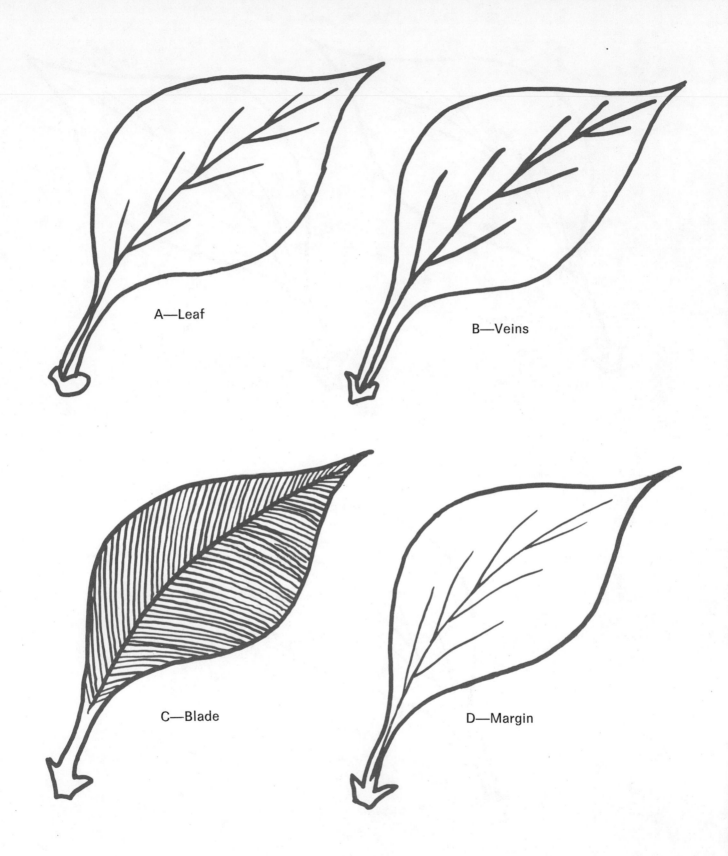

A—Leaf

B—Veins

C—Blade

D—Margin

Fig. 28 — Botany Cards—Leaf Structure

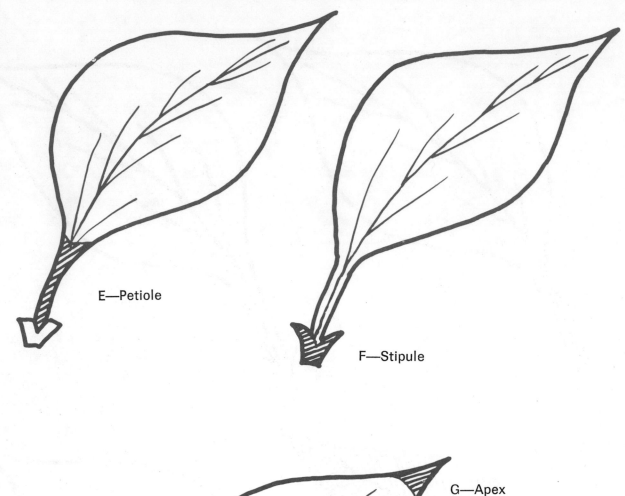

E—Petiole

F—Stipule

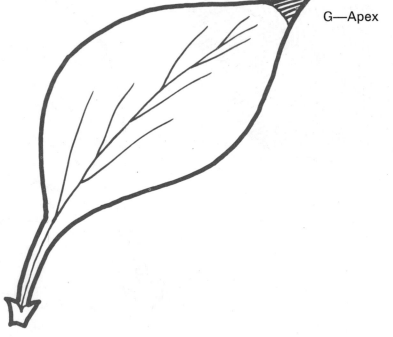

G—Apex

Fig. 28 — Botany Cards—Leaf Structure

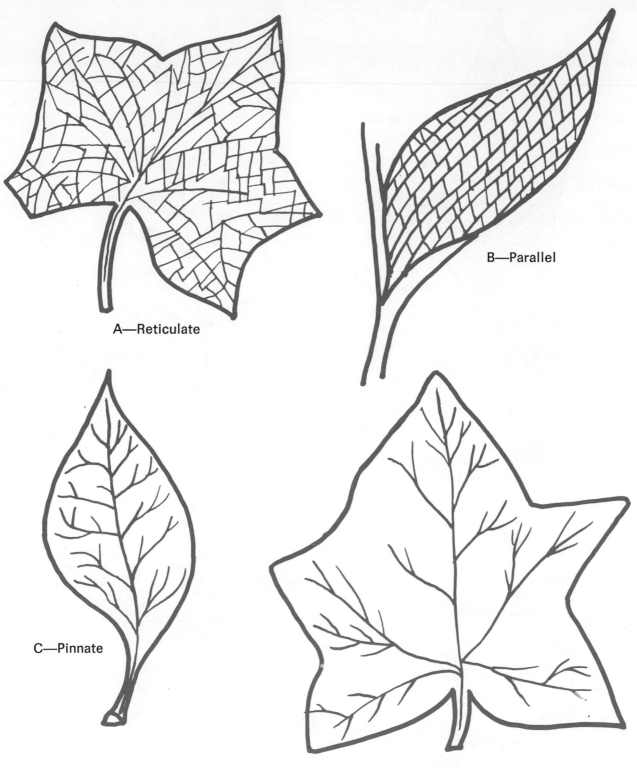

A—Reticulate

B—Parallel

C—Pinnate

D—Palmate

Fig. 29 — Botany Cards—Leaf Veins

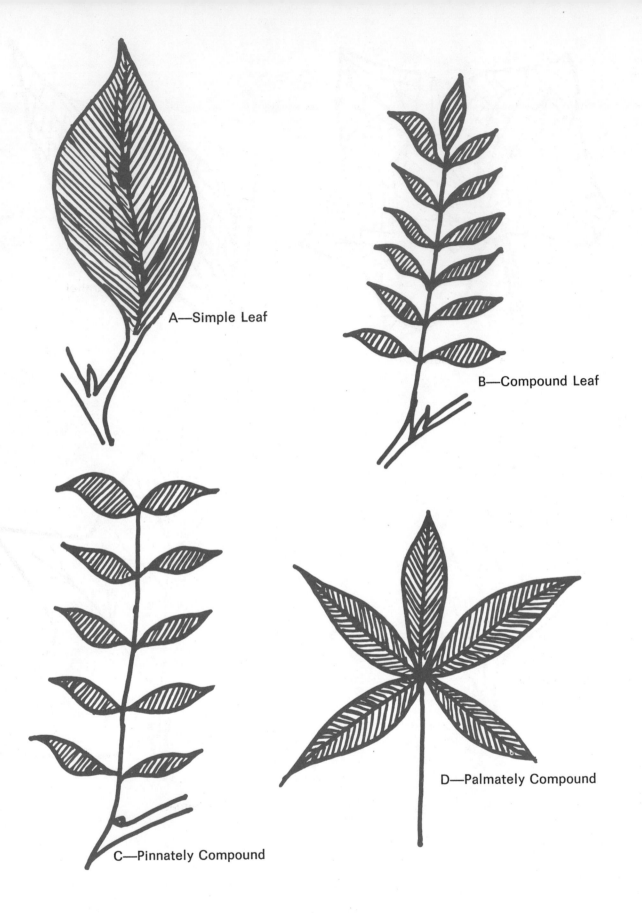

A—Simple Leaf

B—Compound Leaf

C—Pinnately Compound

D—Palmately Compound

Fig. 30 — Botany Cards—Leaf Blades

50

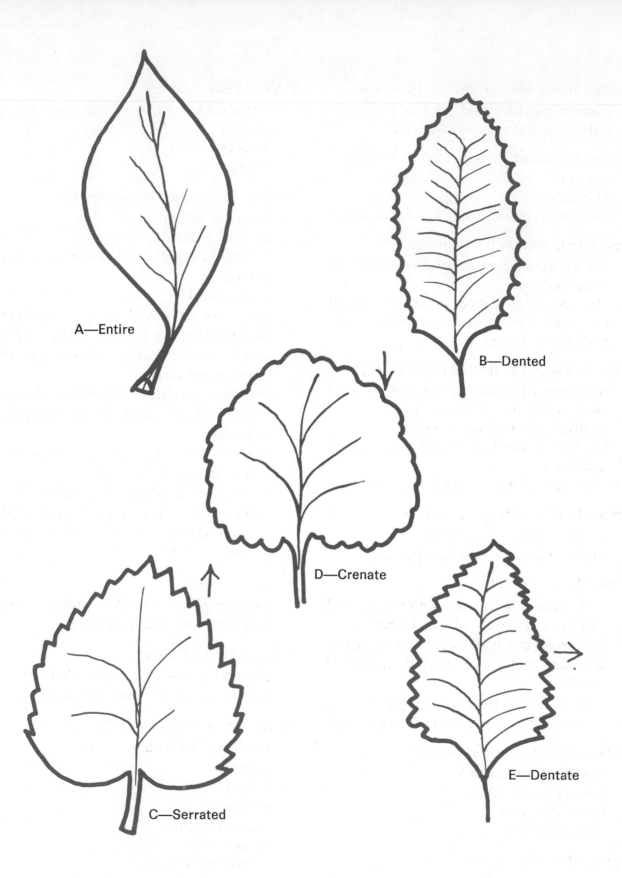

A—Entire

B—Dented

D—Crenate

C—Serrated

E—Dentate

Fig. 31 — Botany Cards—Leaf Margins

51

Dented margins may also be classified:
    pinnately (also lobed, fid, sect)
    palmately (also lobed, fid, sect)

Leaves Classified by Attachment to Stem
    opposite
    alternate
    whorled (coming from a central point)

Root Cards and their Language
    fasciculated—generally fibrous and all
    alike (grass)
    tap—descends deeply into the ground
    and generally produces branches (oak,
    wallflower, bean)

Tap roots may be classified as follows:
    napiform (globular at top and tapering
    off abruptly as a turnip or beet)
    conical (resembling a cone)
    fusiform (tapering toward each end, as
    a radish)
    tuberous (fleshy, shaped like a tuber)

Stem Cards and their Language
    aerial—above the ground
    subterranean—below the ground

Basic Parts of a Stem
    axil (angle between a branch or leaf
    and the axis from which it arises)
    axil bud (the bud located at the axil)
    terminal bud (bud located at end of
    stem)
    node (thick area where leaf joins stem)
    internode (the area between the nodes)

Types of Subterranean Stems
    corm (like a crocus)
    bulb (like an onion)
    tuber (potato)
    rhizome (iris)

Types of Aerial Stems
    erect
    climbing
    procumbent

Types of Erect Stems
    herbaceous (green, lives only for a
    season)
    shrubby
    woody

Flower Cards and their Language
    complete flower
    parts of a flower:
    calyx—external green leafy part, cup-
    shaped
    corolla—petals
    pistil—contains the ovary (seed-box)
    and the stigma, a spongy, sticky surface
    which catches pollen. Seeds are ma-
    tured in the pistil
    stamen — contains the male element
    where pollen is produced in the anther
    or pocket
    pollen — a dusty-appearing substance
    which causes seeds to grow
    style—a thread-like prolongation of a
    plant ovary, bearing a stigma at its apex
    stigma—the part of the pistil which re-
    ceives the pollen

Types of Calyx
    gamosepalous—complete, not divided
    polysepalous—many-petalled

Position of the Calyx
    hypogynous—calyx under seed box
    epigynous—calyx over the seed box

Shapes of Gamopetalous Corolla
    rotate (wheel-like)
    spurred
    tubular
    labiate
    hypocrateriform
    liqulate (like a belt)
    urceolate (urn-like)
    personate (like pursed lips)
    imbutiform (funnel-shaped)
    companulate (bell-shaped)

A—Opposite

B—Alternate

C—Whorled

Fig. 32 — Botany Cards—Attachment of Leaf to Stem

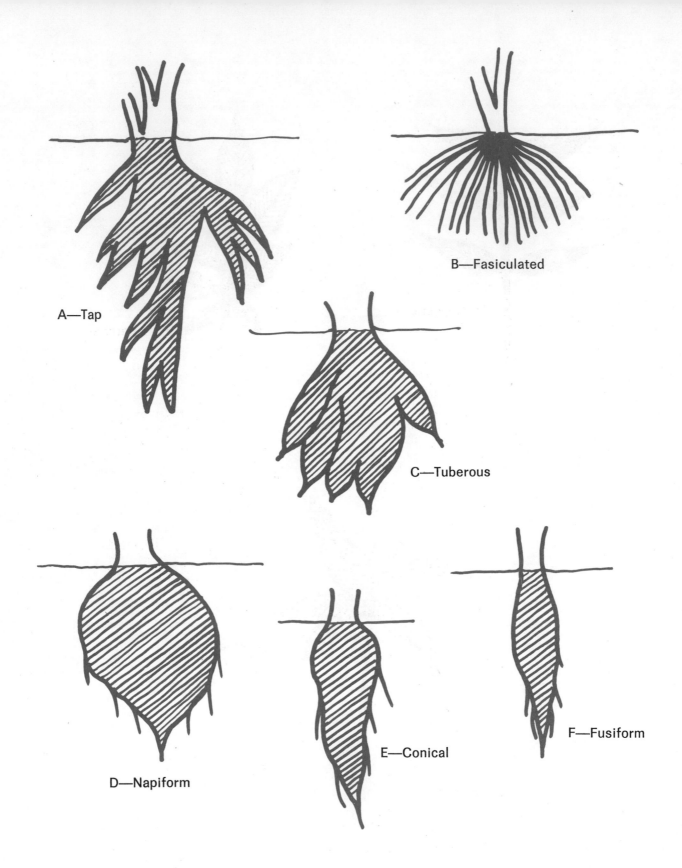

A—Tap

B—Fasiculated

C—Tuberous

D—Napiform

E—Conical

F—Fusiform

Fig. 33 —Botany Cards—Roots

54

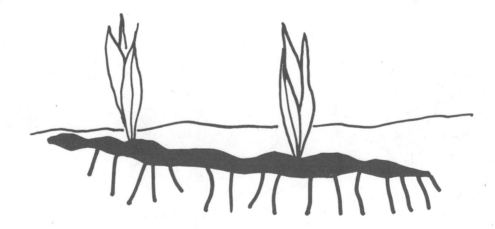

A—Aerial

B—Subterranean

Fig. 34 — Botany Cards—Types of Stems

55

A—Axil

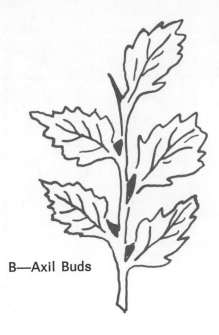

B—Axil Buds

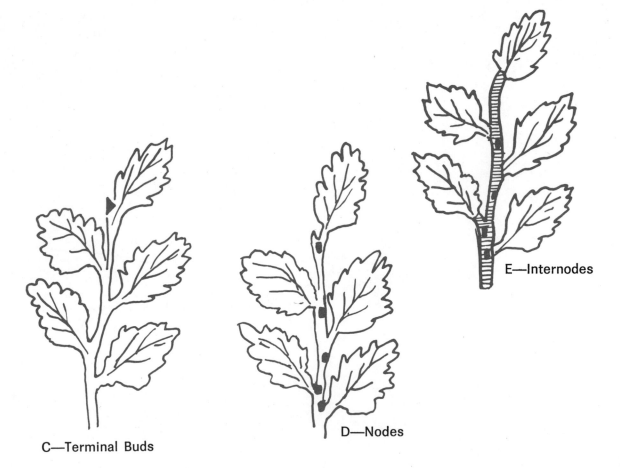

C—Terminal Buds

D—Nodes

E—Internodes

Fig. 35 — Botany Cards—Basic Parts of Stem

56

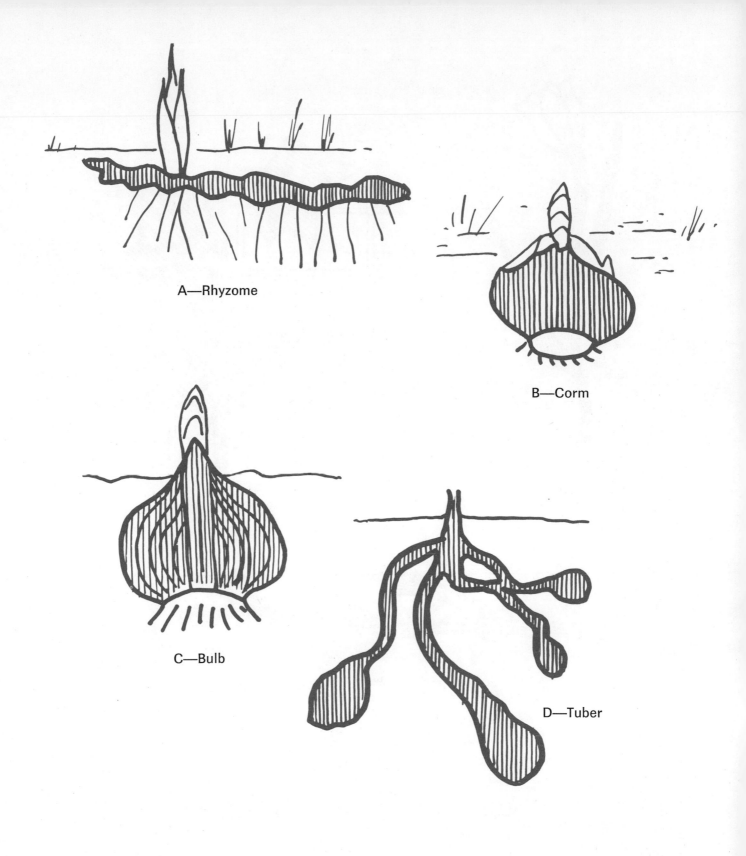

A—Rhyzome

B—Corm

C—Bulb

D—Tuber

Fig. 36 — Botany Cards—Subterranean Stems

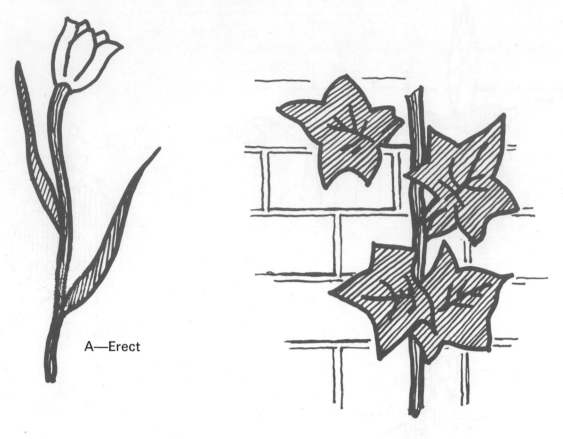

A—Erect

B—Climbing

C—Procumbent

Fig. 37 — Botany Cards—Aerial Stems

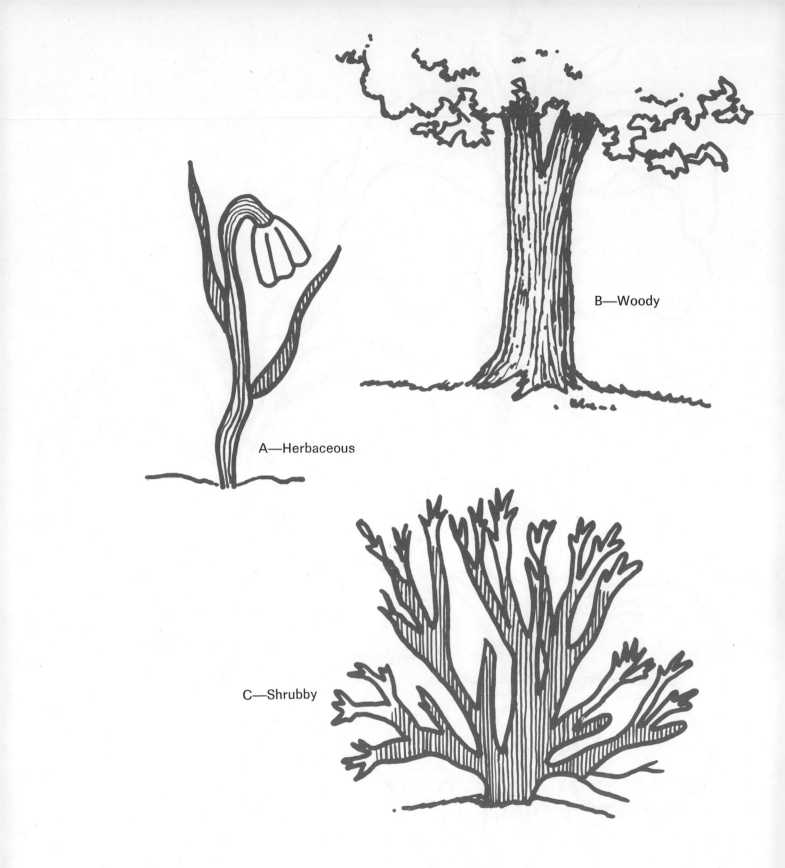

A—Herbaceous

B—Woody

C—Shrubby

Fig. 38 —Botany Cards—Types of Erect Stems

59

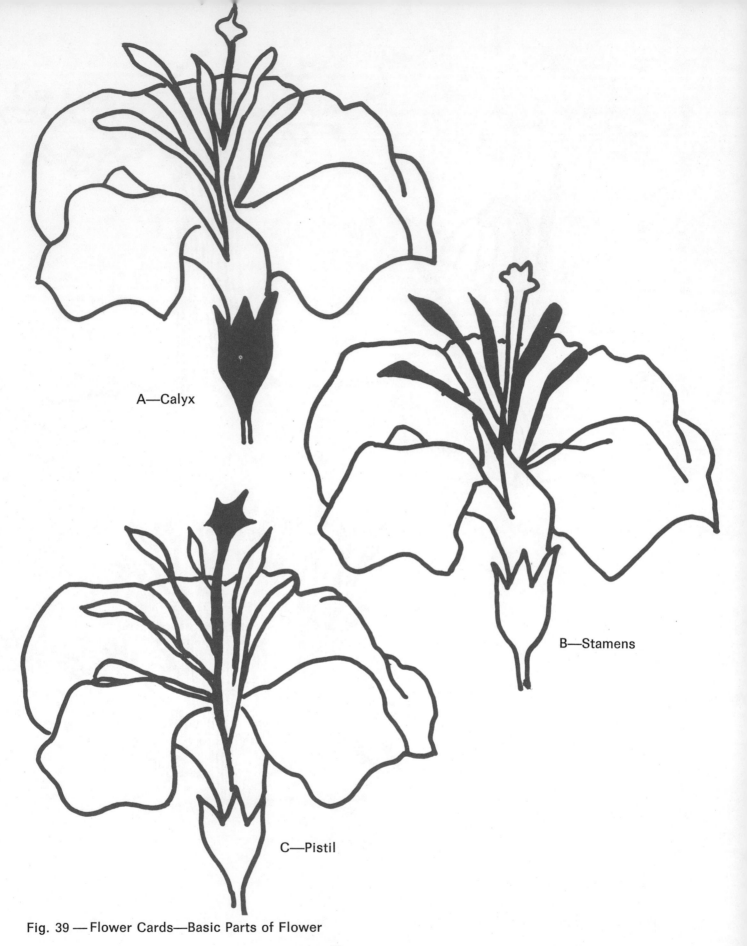

A—Calyx

B—Stamens

C—Pistil

Fig. 39 — Flower Cards—Basic Parts of Flower

60

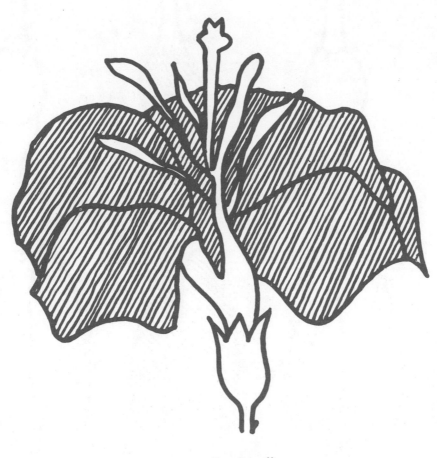

D—Corolla

Fig. 39

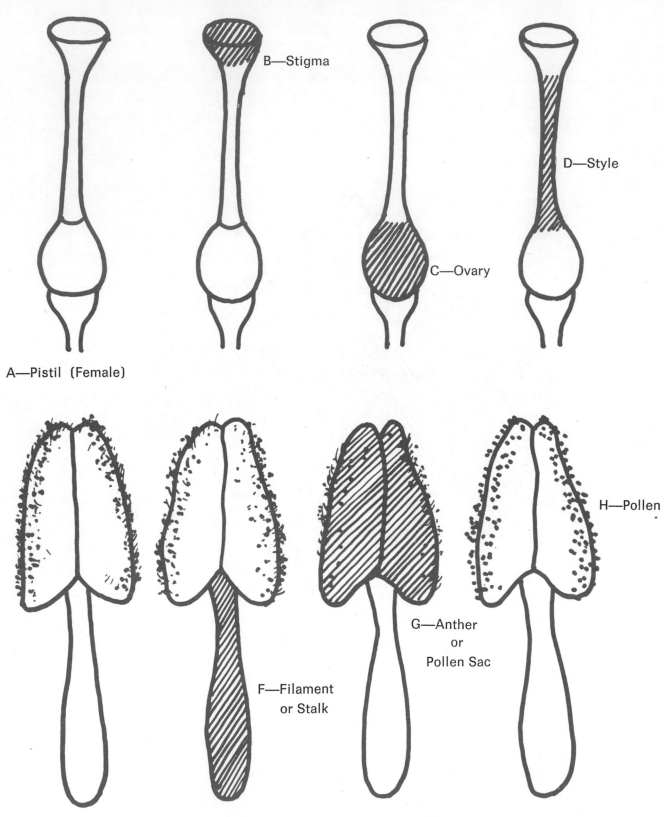

B—Stigma

D—Style

C—Ovary

A—Pistil (Female)

H—Pollen

G—Anther
or
Pollen Sac

F—Filament
or Stalk

E—Stamen (Male)

Fig. 40 — Flower Cards—Pistil and Stamen

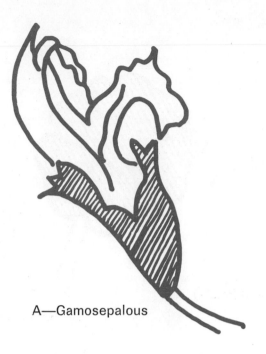

A—Gamosepalous

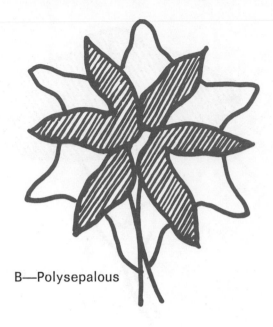

B—Polysepalous

C—Hypogynous (Under Seed Box)

D—Epignous (Over Seed Box)

Fig. 41 — Flower Cards—Types and Position of Calyx

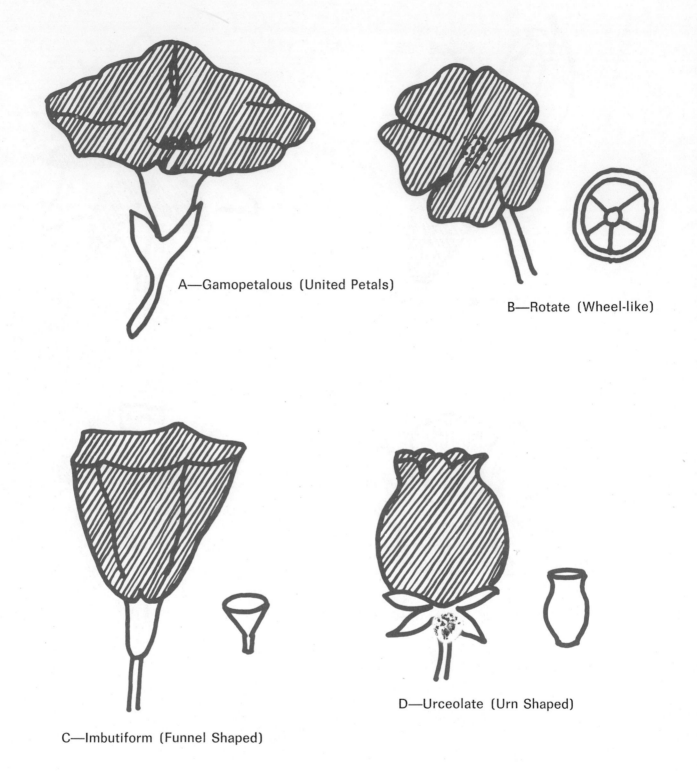

A—Gamopetalous (United Petals)

B—Rotate (Wheel-like)

C—Imbutiform (Funnel Shaped)

D—Urceolate (Urn Shaped)

Fig. 42 — Flower Cards—Shapes of Gamopetalous Corolla

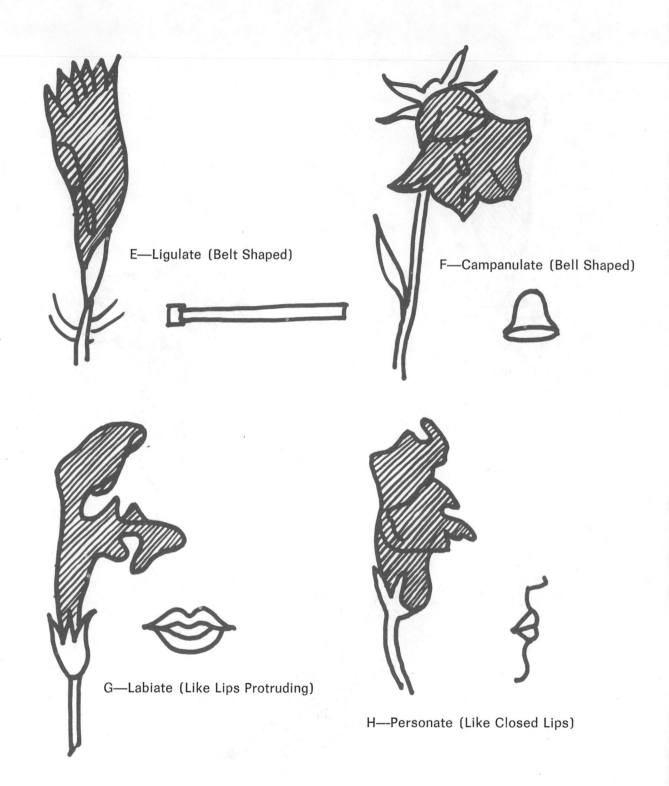

E—Ligulate (Belt Shaped)

F—Campanulate (Bell Shaped)

G—Labiate (Like Lips Protruding)

H—Personate (Like Closed Lips)

Fig. 42

65

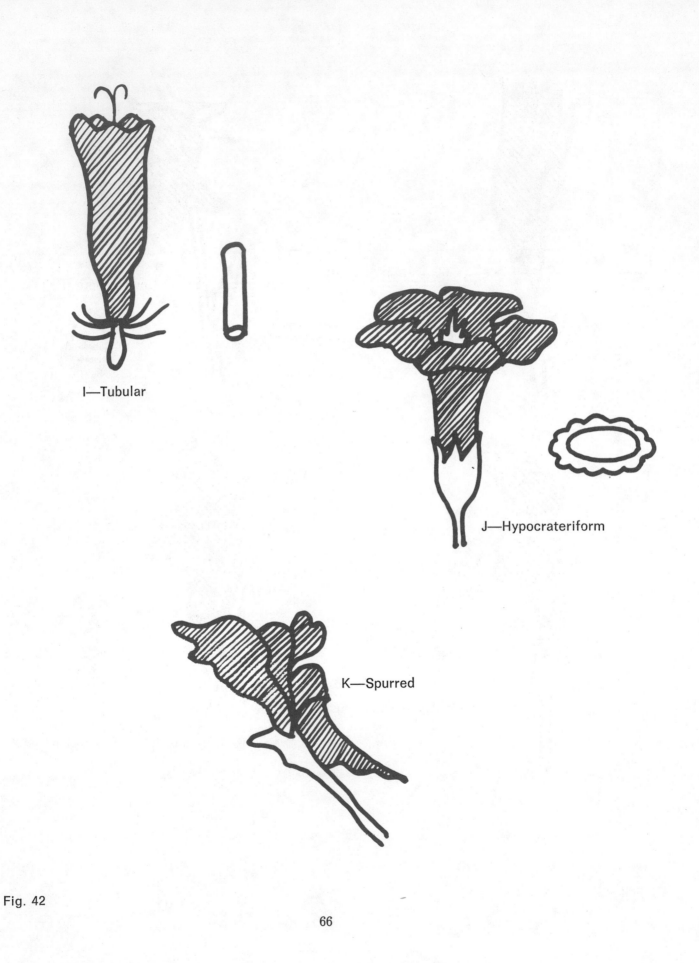

I—Tubular

J—Hypocrateriform

K—Spurred

Fig. 42

66

Shapes of Polypetalous Corolla
   rotate
   cruciform (like a cross)
   papilionaceous (like a butterfly)

Attachment of Flowers to Stem
   raceme—attached along entire stem by
   distinct stalks
   corymb—attached to one particular
   point, as a flat-topped cluster
   spike—attached directly along the stem
   head—stalkless flowers bunched com-
   pactly, attached directly to stem
   umbel—a cluster in which stalks appear
   to rise from the same level
   panicle—a compound raceme

Fruit Cards and their Language
   Dry fruit
      silique
      follicle
      legume
      capsule

   Succulent fruit
      composite (pineapple)
      aggregate (berry)
      pome (apple)
      drupe (peach)
      pepo (melon)

Presentation of Botany Cards

Prereading stage (Card with no name on it)

Use this card in connection with child's
own exploration. Either bring in specimens
or go outside and find samples. Always
point out one thing at a time.

AIM

To provide a key to exploration. To give
the child a point of consciousness.

AGE

3½ years onwards.

LANGUAGE

The names (listed above) are to be
taught as the child goes along and in connection with the actual thing.

Reading stage

One set of botany cards without names.

One set with names below and separate
name slips in the envelope. These are used
in reading. First the child pairs the cards
only. Then he pairs the words. Later he
will be able to place a picture in front of
him, find and read the separate word and
place it in the space provided. He then reads
the word on the appropriate picture and
pairs this with the separate word and picture.

AGE

5½ to 6 years onwards.

Classified Picture Cards

A double set of boxed picture cards of
flowers and plants. They are grouped according to whether they are gamopetalous
or polypetalous and also according to color.

PRESENTATION

The child first pairs the pictures, as
with the geography cards. Later, teach the
language by the three-period lesson.

Experiments

Botanical experiments in the classroom
must be simple, represent a basic fact and
be quickly completed. Our aim is to demonstrate basic facts, not explain why things
happen. A few are listed. The directress
should find many more.

EXPERIMENTS WITH GERMINATION

In container "A" place soil, beans or
seeds, moisten with water and place in a
light area.

In container "B," set seeds or beans the
same way, but place where there is no
light. Place a thick black paper around the
container. After a few days, observe the

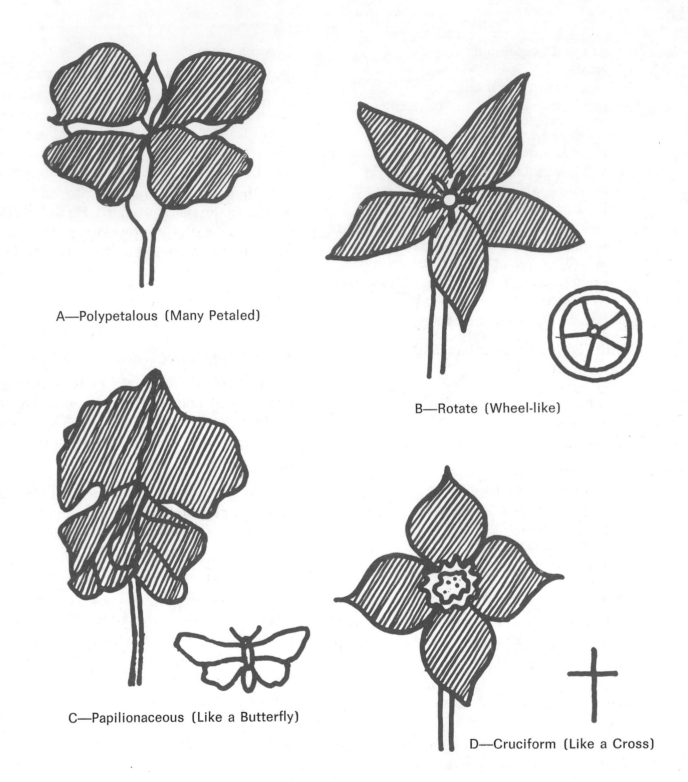

A—Polypetalous (Many Petaled)

B—Rotate (Wheel-like)

C—Papilionaceous (Like a Butterfly)

D—Cruciform (Like a Cross)

Fig. 43 — Flower Cards—Shapes of Polypetalous Corolla

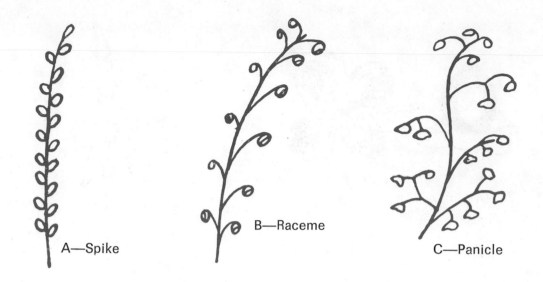

A—Spike   B—Raceme   C—Panicle

D—Umbel   E—Corymb   F—Head

Fig. 44 —Flower Cards—Attachment of Flowers to Stem

A—Dry Fruit—Nut

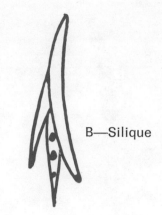

B—Silique

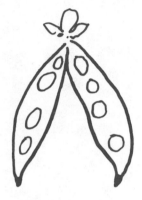

C—Legume

D—Capsules

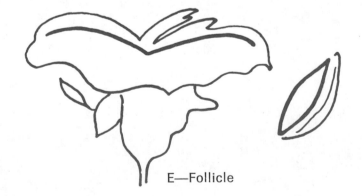

E—Follicle

Fig. 45 —Fruit Cards—Dry

70

Stone

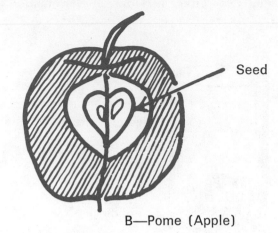
Seed

A—Drupe (Peach)

B—Pome (Apple)

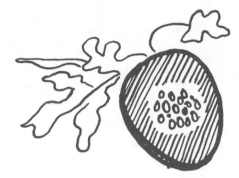

C—Pepo (Melon)

D—Berry

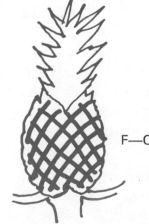
F—Composite

E—Aggregate

Fig. 46 — Fruit Cards—Succulent

Fig. 47 — Effect of Light on Germination

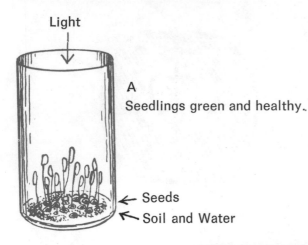

Light

A
Seedlings green and healthy.

Seeds

Soil and Water

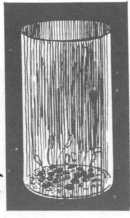

B
Seedlings white
and spindly.

Black Paper
No Light

Seeds →
Soil and Water →

Fig. 48 — Effect of Water on Germination

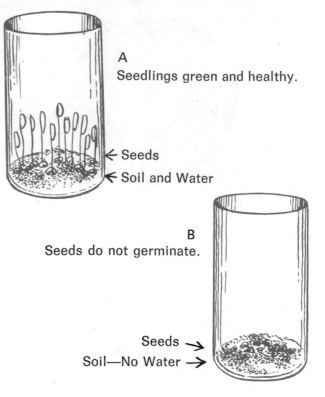

A
Seedlings green and healthy.

Seeds

Soil and Water

B
Seeds do not germinate.

Seeds →
Soil—No Water →

Fig. 49 — Effect of Food on Germination

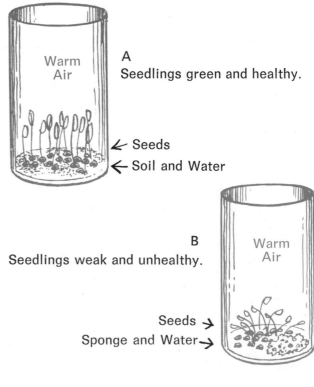

Warm
Air

A
Seedlings green and healthy.

Seeds

Soil and Water

B
Seedlings weak and unhealthy.

Warm
Air

Seeds →
Sponge and Water →

results. Both will have sprouted, but "A" sprouts are green and healthy, while "B" sprouts are white and spindly.

AIM

To demonstrate the need for light.

Prepare containers as in experiment number 1, but omit water from container "B." Keep both containers on the nature table for several days. Observe results. Seeds do not germinate in container "B," but will germinate in "A."

AIM

To demonstrate that plants need water.

Prepare two containers and set with seeds. Container "A" has soil, warmth, air and water. Container "B" has seeds set on a sponge or flannel, but also has warmth, air and water.

72

Fig. 50 — Effect of Temperature on Germination

Fig. 51 — Effect of Temperature and Light on Plants

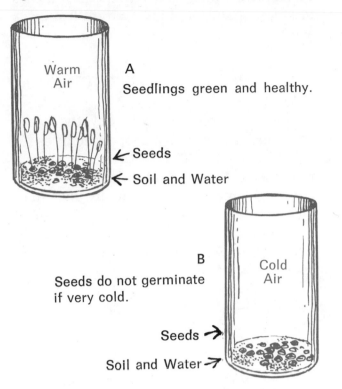

Warm Air

A
Seedlings green and healthy.

← Seeds
← Soil and Water

B
Seeds do not germinate if very cold.

Cold Air

Seeds →
Soil and Water →

A
Plant on sunny windowsill—green and healthy.

B—Plant in shade—tall in search of light.

C—Plant in cold has little growth.

After a few days the seeds will germinate but the sprouts in container "A" will be healthy. Those in container "B" will be weak and unhealthy.

AIM

To show that plants need food.

Plant seeds in exactly the same way. Give each plant soil, water and air. Place container "A" where air is warm. Place container "B" in a refrigerator or other cold place. After several days, observe results. The seeds in container "A" germinate, while those in container "B" do not.

AIM

To demonstrate that plants (seeds) need warmth to germinate. Similar experiments may be set up to show the effect of light and cold on plants.

Plant broad beans in three separate containers giving each the necessary food, moisture, light and warmth. After they have come up, put one on a sunny windowsill, another in a shady spot, and a third in the refrigerator.

The bean in the sun will grow slowly but sturdily, and have green leaves.

The bean plant in the shade will grow a tall stem, as it seeks the light. The leaves may be small.

The plant in the refrigerator will grow very little.

AIM

To demonstrate that plants need. warmth and light.

Books and Stories

The book corner in the prepared environment should have beautifully illustrated nature books showing different plants, leaves, flowers, roots, and stems. These give the child practice in reading and additional botanical information. He may compare the book illustrations with the materials of the leaf cabinet and botany cards, also he may compare it with natural specimens. Good reference materials are necessary for both the child and the directress. They stimulate interest and provide reading practice.

Handwork

The leaf insets may be traced by the child and colored with crayons, paint or sticky paper. Leaf specimens may be collected, blotted and dried. These may then be pressed and mounted later. Children may wish to draw leaf shapes of plants and flowers free hand, and then color them.

Zoology

The world of animals is divided into vertebrates and invertebrates. As they are part of the world about him, the child should be helped to bring some order and clarity to his experiences with animals. The families of invertebrates are numerous and their structure is not so easy for little children to understand. We can capture insects and observe them from time to time, however. Our emphasis is on the vertebrates which have five main branches to study—fish, amphibians, reptiles, birds and mammals.

PREPARATION OF THE ENVIRONMENT

The directress should study the needs of animals and arrange proper facilities for them, before introducing them into the environment. She should begin by having only one animal and gradually introduce more. Animals may be either permanent pets or visitors to the classroom. During the year, the child should have the opportunity to study representatives of the five branches of vertebrates and also some of the invertebrates.

It is recommended that all schools have a cold water aquarium for *fish*.

Amphibians should be visitors only. They are difficult to maintain and feed in captivity.

To represent the *reptile* family, a tortoise can be a permanent feature. He needs warm water. The child can observe hibernation during the winter.

Birds can easily be attracted by having a bird feeder in the garden or placing food on the windowsill.

Mammals may be either permanent pets or come as visitors. Guinea pigs make excellent pets, as they are clean, have no odor and can be quite affectionate. Hamsters are also suitable. Many children have pets at home and can bring them to visit for a day.

The invertebrates may be represented by having a wormery, so the child can observe the life of worms in different soils. Silkworms on mulberry leaves, stick-insects in jars, and ant farms can also be studied in the classroom. An interesting thing to do is place a snail on a sheet of glass and observe it from underneath.

EXERCISES OF PRACTICAL LIFE

Caring for the animals should be a privilege not a right. That privilege should be taken away without question, if the child in any way abuses or mishandles the animal. Some of the activities of practical life to teach the child are how to:

Feed the animals

Handle the animals properly

Clean the cage, fish bowl, or other home

Give the animals water to drink

SENSORIAL KEYS

For each animal you have, there should be a set of *classified animal cards,* marking the main parts of the body. This material provides a sensorial link with the animals of the environment.

Use in prereading stage as classified pictures. The child merely pairs them.

In the reading stage he uses them first as any other classified reading card.

1st place picture without name.

2nd match picture having name on bottom.

3rd place picture with name and sound out the name. Match separate name slip. Place corresponding picture.

4th read separate name slip. Find picture and place it by the name.

Two sets of classified pictures of different branches of the vertebrates should be collected by the directress and kept in the classroom. The child matches the pictures one set at a time, then all sets together. Later you teach him the names. Field visits to the zoo are another way of linking the sensorial material to the environment.

LANGUAGE

Amphibians—Any of a class of cold-blooded vertebrates, intermediate between fish and reptiles. They are able to live both on land and in water (frog, salamander, newt).

Reptiles—Any of a class of air-breathing vertebrates that crawls or moves on its belly or short legs (lizards, snakes, turtle, alligator).

Fish—A cold-blooded aquatic animal with an elongated body, generally tapering off to a tail.

Birds—Any of a class of warm-blooded vertebrates distinguished by having the body more or less completely covered with feathers and the forelimbs modified as wings.

Mammals—Any of a class of higher vertebrates comprising man and all other animals that nourish their young with milk secreted by mammary glands and have the skin more or less covered with hair (horse, deer, rabbit, dog).

BOOKS AND STORIES

The book corner should contain well-illustrated books and stories based on scientific information about animals. These will increase the child's knowledge and stimulate interest in animals.

Art

Montessori classrooms have received some criticism for the absence of creative activities for the child. It has been said that by stressing the need for precision and order the imagination and creative impulses of the child are blocked. A close examination shows such comments to be unfounded. Dr. Montessori emphasized the importance of educating the senses as a means of intellectual development. We try to help the child know what he sees, not just give him more to look at. Dr. Montessori states that by preparing the hand and the senses, natural aid is given not only to writing but to expressive drawing. "We do not teach drawing by drawing, however, but by providing the opportunity to prepare the instruments of expression."[6]

---

[6]Maria Montessori, *The Discovery of the Child* (Madras, India: Kalakshetra Publications, 1962), p. 345.

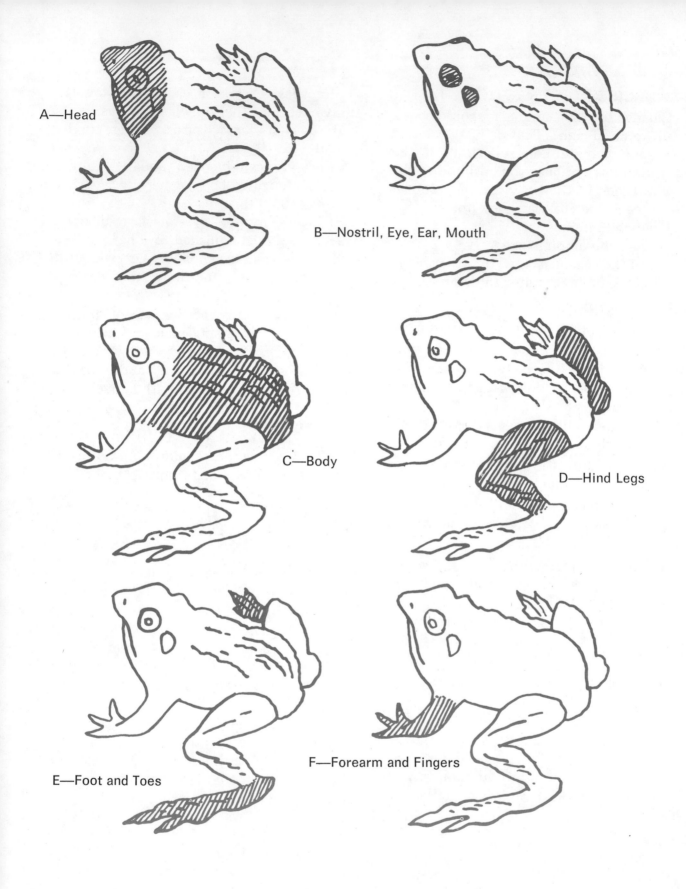

A—Head

B—Nostril, Eye, Ear, Mouth

C—Body

D—Hind Legs

E—Foot and Toes

F—Forearm and Fingers

Fig. 52 — Zoology Cards—Main Parts of Frog

Fig. 53 — Main Parts of Tortoise

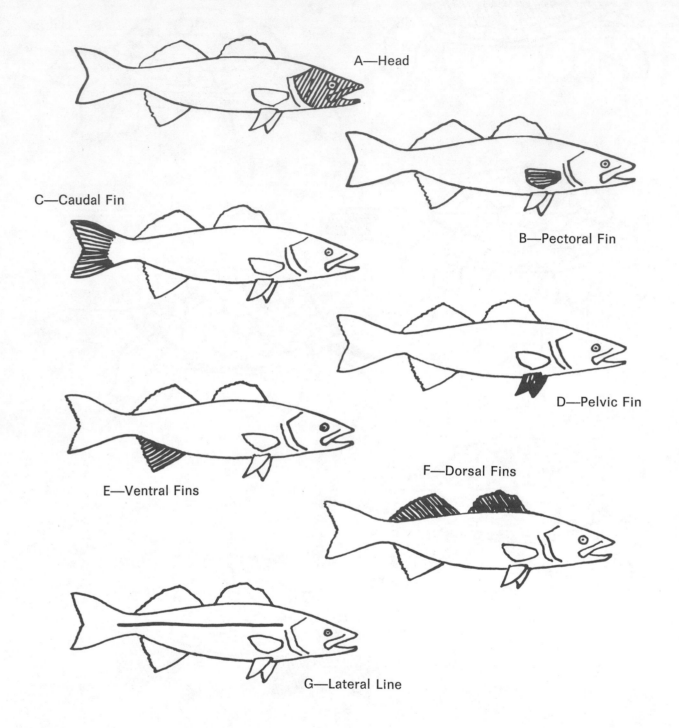

A—Head

C—Caudal Fin

B—Pectoral Fin

D—Pelvic Fin

E—Ventral Fins

F—Dorsal Fins

G—Lateral Line

Fig. 54 — Zoology Cards—Main Parts of Fish

A—Head

B—Beak

C—Wing

D—Tail

E—Legs

F—Claws

Fig. 55 — Zoology Cards — Main Parts of Bird

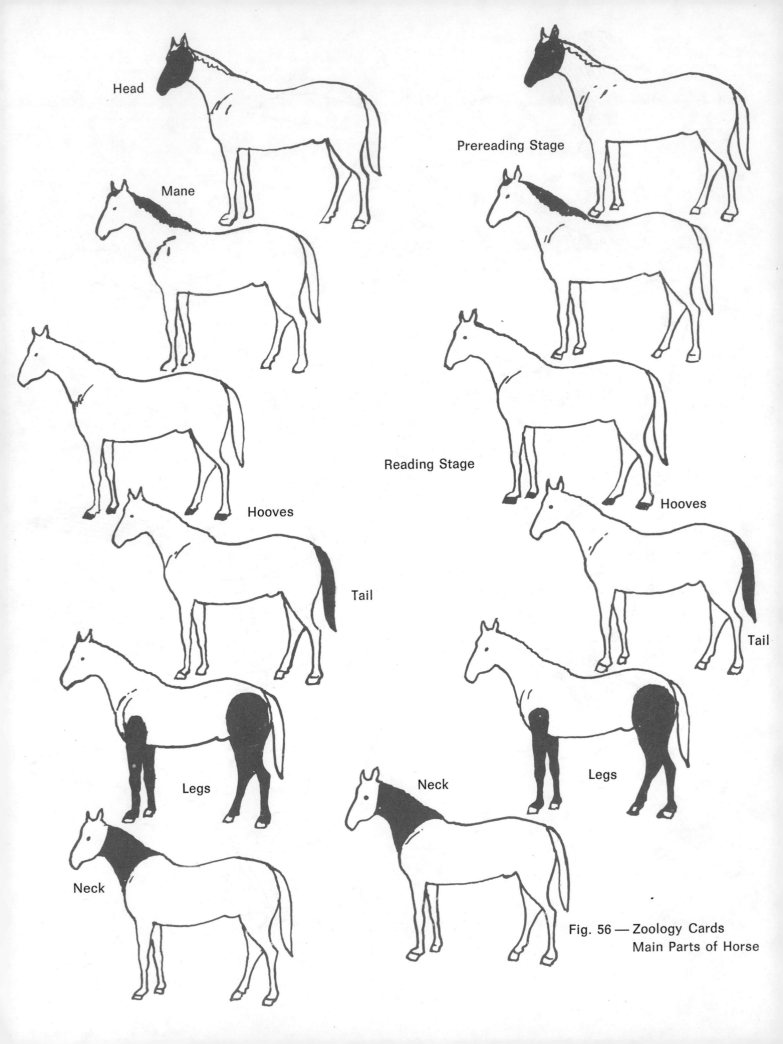

Head

Prereading Stage

Mane

Reading Stage

Hooves

Hooves

Tail

Tail

Legs

Legs

Neck

Neck

Fig. 56 — Zoology Cards
Main Parts of Horse

Montessori schools aim to assist the child by giving him basic techniques and then allowing him to create artistically according to his own feelings. Indirect preparation for later self-expression is provided through a variety of media. Art and handwork broaden the meaning and understanding of whatever subject is taught. The prepared environment includes easily accessible equipment. The apparatus is purposely limited to provide some additional area of social development. He quickly learns to wait his turn at the easel and to leave the materials in good order for the next person.

The room itself should be attractive. Framed or matted reproductions of great painters should be hung on the wall at child's eye-level, fresh flowers and growing plants in good looking containers also beautify the environment.

PRACTICAL LIFE EXERCISES

Some suggestions are listed below. Opportunities are endless.

Cleaning paint from floor and easel after use.

Sweeping up after cutting paper.

Washing the table after clay modeling.

Replacing materials on art shelf.

Washing hands.

Use aprons and hang them up after use.

SENSORIAL KEYS

What is it that makes one appreciate an oil painting, water color, sculpture or other work of art? Each piece contains the three basic elements of design, composition and balance. The Montessori school seeks to develop the child's appreciation of these qualities by specific help as follows:

Order in the environment (everything has its place and must be returned). Equipment kept in good repair.

Observation and memory is helped by his work with the sensorial apparatus—prisms, cylinders, geometric shapes and solids, touch boards, sorting and grading exercises, fabric boxes, and the leaf cabinet.

Sense of form and color are also developed through the sensorial apparatus. The color tablets develop the chromatic sense. Pairing, grading, memorizing and matching the colors in the tablets to things in the environment develops his powers of observation.

The geometric cabinet gives points of consciousness to the child. He learns the shapes first by feeling and replacing. Later, he tries to find the shapes in his environment. This develops observation.

The metal insets, used first individually and then superimposed develop muscular coordination and also powers of observation.

The wooden geometric patterns, large and small, teach control of the paint brush and develop the child's sense of form.

Sandpaper letters, actual writing and manipulating the pencil, tracing maps and leaf shapes, develop technical skill.

Classified art pictures are postcard size reproductions of great paintings. One set is grouped according to subject matter, the other is grouped according to the artist's country or school.

The entire field of sense education is basic to Montessori teaching but space does not permit a detailed discussion here. Descriptions and instructions on the use of sensorial apparatus may be found in a number of Montessori books. (See Bibliography.)

PREPARATION OF THE ENVIRONMENT

In addition to having an orderly and attractive environment containing sensorial keys the directress should also provide:

An art shelf where materials are freely available

Mats to protect the floor

Easel for painting

Blackboard and colored chalk for large drawing work. (Large movements come first, just as in practical life.)

Plastic aprons or old shirts to be used as smocks

A separate table for modeling and plastic clay work

Suggested list for storage cupboard:

Strong, sturdy paper such as butcher paper for painting

Smooth paper for drawings and more precise work

Construction paper

Scraps for collage work

Paint—premixed with water

Tempera blocks for use when the child begins to mix his own colors

Wax crayons

Colored pencils

Colored chalk

Soft drawing pencils

Soft erasers

Charcoal and a spray fixative

Glue, paste and brushes

Paint brushes (firm and flat for beginners)—hog or sable bristles

Clay kept fresh in airtight container and plastic bag

Blunt-end scissors

Plastic clay

BASIC TECHNIQUES

Painting

MATERIALS NEEDED

Mat for floor, single easel and board with large clips.

Holder for paint pots, cleaning cloth and a bowl for cleaning up.

Three small pots of premixed primary colors and a brush in each. Show the child how to hold the brush, wipe excess off the jar, and apply the paint to the paper. A large paper is best for beginners up to 4 years old. After 4 years old (about) the child can work with tempera block colors. He needs only one brush, a pot of water and a clean saucer. Show him how to mix colors, rinse his brush and change water often.

GEOMETRIC PATTERNS

The basic geometric shapes in wood, each in a large and a smaller size. The square is 15″ x 15″ and there also is an 8″ square. The directress draws the outline in wax crayon and has a choice available in the classroom. The child fills inside the shape with one color, outside with another. Eventually, he traces his own and makes designs. Other shapes are the triangle, rectangle, circle and pentagon. Metal insets, fraction insets, leaf shapes and maps may be used similarly after the child gains experience.

OTHER PAINT ACTIVITIES

Combine paint and charcoal or paint and wax crayons. Paint over a white wax design on white paper is interesting. Make a color chart. See how many shades the child can mix from red, yellow and blue. The child should be introduced to the basic techniques of painting and given ample opportunity to practice them. As he grows through experience, he will gradually develop some ability to express himself through his painting. This can only be done through letting him choose his subjects and colors freely.

AGE

3 to 4 years onwards.

Paper Activities

MATERIALS

Glue, brush, scissors, newspaper to protect table, construction paper, colored tissue, colored magazines, cellophane, miscellaneous scraps of papers, string, sequins and dry leaves.

Tearing method: filling an outline. Teacher draws a large circle using the wooden pattern. Have the child tear colored paper into bits and fill in the circle. Use only 3-5 colors for balance.

Folding and cutting: after child can use a scissors, ruler and compass, demonstrate single folds to make leaves, trees, valentines and other figures. Band patterns can be made by using double and multiple folds for stars, wheels, snowflakes, et cetera. Pictures, patterns and group work can be built up from these.

Child can draw his own picture, cut it out and applique it to a larger sheet for background color.

Mosaics and collage work can be done in a decorative or representational way or can be related to the cultural subjects. The child cuts stamp-size colored strips from magazines, and cloth fabrics. He draws design on paper and glues in the colored materials.

AGE

3 to 6 years, approximately.

Drawing

Wax crayons on smooth paper. Use thick, large crayons and large paper. Encourage large arm movements. Show how to hold crayon and overlay colors to make a new color.

Charcoal or pastels—A fixative is needed to prevent smudging. Charcoal should be about 2″ lengths. Show child how to hold the charcoal lightly and to keep his arm and hand away from the paper. Charcoal is only black, so show him how to give texture and depth to his drawings by rubbing charcoal sideways, making dots, swirls, and short lines. Pastels come in a variety of colors and techniques are similar.

Colored pencils — A smooth paper is needed and a sharpener or sandpaper. Light colors over darker ones, shaded in opposite direction, produce lovely tones. Trace insets, leaf shapes, maps, et cetera. Illustrate stories from books. Give the child an idea of one or two writing patterns. Let him develop his own ideas. These activities provide later help for writing techniques.

AGE

4 years onwards.

Printing

MATERIALS

Paint, brush, and sponge or felt to make a pad. Newspaper for experimenting, and smooth, absorbent paper for prints. Show the child how to apply paint with his brush to the pad. Place a potato block or other object to be printed firmly onto the pad. Print the design on colored or plain paper.

Prints can be made from an unlimited variety of materials and used the same way. Cork, leaves, brushes, artificial flowers, and pieces of sponge are a few suggestions. Kitchen cupboards are a good source of supply. Twist a piece of cotton around a few dried peas, rice or beans for an interesting texture effect. Make string blocks for printing by gluing a swirl, zig-zag or other shape of string onto a block of linoleum or cardboard. Cut simple shapes out of felt and glue onto a block for printing. Potato blocks are easy to make. Cut the potato straight in half. Let child print with this or cut his own design in the middle.

AGE

3 to 4 years onwards.

Fig. 58 — Clay Modeling

A—Building coil pot

B—Balls of clay pinched to shape

C—Building slab pot

Fig. 57 — Potato Block Printing

Modeling

MATERIALS

Apron or smock, wooden board covered with oil cloth, fabric side up, water, clay kept in airtight bucket and covered with plastic, a wire for cutting, rolling pin, spoon.

PRESENTATION

Show how to roll a ball, make a "snake" coil, and a flat pancake (flatten a ball). Let child experiment.

METHODS

Model animals or bowls by first shaping a ball, then pinch out legs and head. A bowl is formed by pinching out a hole in the middle and gradually pressing out the sides.

Coil pots or animals start with a flat pancake as a base. Make coils and wind around to shape the sides. Place one coil on top of another and weld together by pressing with wet spoon.

Slab pots and houses are made by first rolling out clay to about ¼″ thickness using a rolling pin. Cut out rectangle for walls, base and roof. Roughen the edge where you will attach one slab to the other and moisten both pieces before connecting them.

Geography models of the land forms can best be made out of plastic modeling clay, as it is water repellent. You need a rectangular pie tin about 6″ x 8″ for each landform (see geography).

First, press an outline strip of modeling material firmly and smoothly onto the bottom of the pan. Crumple newspaper and form into desired shape. Place this within the outline. Hold the newspapers in place, while building up plastic strips around it. Cover the entire paper mold with plastic strips. Seal the edges and give final touches. Build land formations relatively high and steep, so the child can pour water into the water formations and sail a tiny boat.

Sewing and other Handwork

Although needlework in school and at home is not considered so necessary as it was before machine sewing, it is still a most valuable skill. The child should be taught how to hold the scissors and cut the full length of the blade. He can practice cutting by making fringes on paper and paper lanterns.

Muscular coordination leading up to handwork begins with the metal insets. The color tablets and fabric helps give him an appreciation of the use of color and texture in handwork. The sensorial material also provides the repetition and accuracy necessary for handwork. Doll clothes and pattern making is based on mathematical knowledge.

Lacing cards can give the child of 4½ to 5 years practice in the running stitch, climbing stitch, overcasting and the buttonhole stitch.

Children can first trace designs from the metal insets, then use flower patterns, Christmas trees, et cetera, to make patterns, then stitch them by hand. A choice of handwork should always be available to the child. He might do painting one day and needlework the next.

Classified Cards

Two sets of classified art cards are the history of art grouped by subject matter and then by country, name of painter and his school. Postcard reproductions can be purchased at most art museums by the teacher to build her own collection.

Subject matter cards might be animals, costumes, facial expressions and skies. Lay out one set at a time. Study to see how many ways each subject can be painted. At first, the child will enjoy just laying the cards out and matching them. Later, he can be taught the names.

The cards grouped by country are used as classified reading. One set has no names. One has names attached and also separate. Use one country or school of art at a time. Later mix all the schools and have him sort them. The language taught is the name of the painter, the name of his country and school of painting.

Age

3 years onwards.

Stories and Books

Well-illustrated books on the history of art showing reproductions of famous masters' paintings should be placed in the book corner from time to time. Read and tell about the lives of famous painters or what they were like as children. Hang good reproductions on the wall. Pieces of pottery, sculpture and other works of art may be brought by the teacher and children to share.

Visits to Museums

Children should be taken to see the originals of paintings in their books, cards and the reproductions you hang on the wall, if at all possible. This will help them to realize the reproductions are only pictures of great pictures. In visiting an art gallery or museum with a small child it is important to provide a point of focus. Ask him to see how many different colored skies he can find, how many children, what kinds of fruit, what kinds of animals, birds and buildings.

Music
PREPARATION OF THE ENVIRONMENT

Our environment should have within it the means to develop the child's musical senses and intelligence. This includes making available good quality reproductions of pieces by the great composers and opportunities to listen to live music. The teacher should have good performers visit the class and also take the children to listen to performances. Simple instruments of good quality are also desirable. Children love to hear stories about the lives of the composers. There should be well-illustrated books about them in the book corner.

The Montessori approach to music lies in analyzing each separate part of music —rhythm, harmony writing and reading —so that the child can work with each independently. Only the beginnings of music are taught at an early age. Full development comes later.

SENSORIAL KEYS
The Bells
MATERIAL

A double series of fourteen movable bells representing the tones and semitones of the scale. These are arranged upon a long baseboard on which are painted rectangular black and white spaces of the same size as the base of the bells. As on the piano, the white spaces correspond to the tones and the black to the semitones.

One set of bells (the control) is arranged in chromatic order along the back of the stand. The bases correspond in color to the stand, being either black or white. The second set of bells is of a natural wood base color. These are arranged along the front of the board, opposite their control bells in the back. The bells corresponding to the black are kept separately until they are introduced. There is also a wooden striker.

Fig. 59 — The Bells   —Photo taken at Eugene Montessori School

PRESENTATION
Stage 1

Preliminary, with one bell at the child's table.

1. Show him how to carry the bells by the base or stem. Show him how to hold the striker between the first three fingers. Strike the bell lightly and effortlessly with a sharp flick of the wrist. Strike near the rim of the bell. (Strike near the top to show the difference and emphasize that the rim is the correct place to strike.)

2. Show child how to listen to the bell. Strike bell then hold it near your ear to listen. Say something like, "I can still hear it! Now it's gone." Strike the bell and hold it to the child's ear. Say, "Listen, and tell me when the sound is gone." Show him how to stop the sound with the fingers. Next, ask the child if he'd like to try. Make sure he strikes the bell properly and holds it properly. Allow him to continue as long as he wishes. Show him where the bell "lives" on the board.

EXERCISE 1

Pairing at the child's table. Remove three brown bells of contrasting sound, e.g., C.E.G., and the three matching white bells. Say something like, "Let's see if we can find which brown bell matches the white." Strike a white bell and leave ringing. Strike a brown bell. Stop the sound with fingertips until you strike the matching bell. Always strike the white and allow to ring while searching for the matching brown bell. Set aside each matched pair and continue the process until the three pairs are found. Demonstrate how to replace the bells at the board.

PAIRING PRESENTATION
Stage 2

Invite child to see the bells on the bell board. Play C major scale on white notes, saying "The white notes sound like this." Tell the child the brown bells in front are brothers to the white bells. Play C scale again, slowly, striking the white bell, then its brother. Point to a white bell and ask the child to show you the "brother bell." Strike each in turn. Do this several times with all the bells. The child may try when he understands.

EXERCISE 1

At bell board. Remove three brown bells and mix them up in front of you at the board. Say, "Let's see if we can find the brothers to these three bells." Strike one of the three corresponding white bells and then the first of the three brown bells, listening intently. If they are alike, place the brown bell in its place on the board. If they are not alike, gently stop the brown bell from ringing and set it aside. Again strike the white bell, letting it ring. Then strike the next brown bell. Continue until matched and replace on board. Play the entire scale on the brown bells first, then on the white as a control. Invite the child to try.

EXERCISE 2

Remove all the brown bells and mix. Pair them as in exercise 1. Replace on board. Play entire scale as a control.

GRADING PRESENTATION
Stage 3

Use only the eight neutral colored bells. Mix bells at the board. Look for either the highest or lowest. Strike each bell, stopping the sound, until the lowest is found. Set this aside. Strike this lowest bell, then try to locate the next highest. Always strike your "known" bells in sequence, before striking the next unknown. For example, if you have graded C.D.E. and have set them aside to search for the F sound, strike C.D.E. then the next brown bell. Continue this grading process until the scale is arranged in sequence. Play the scale as a control of error.

GAMES AND ADDITIONAL ACTIVITIES

1. Who would like his name sung? Strike bell in rhythm to the child's name, singing his name up the scale. The next child gets his name sung and played descending the scale. Do this with several children in the group. All sing.

2. Question game. May be done individually but best with a group. The teacher sings "How are you?" and plays G.G.E. on bells. The class answers by singing, "Fine, thank you!" Teacher plays either the same notes again or a lower combination, E.E.C. (Other questions and answers may be used.)

3. Individual singing. Play a simple phrase or the scale and ask who would like to sing it. Go around the class in turn.

4. Grading game. Give one of each of the eight brown bells to each of eight volunteers. Have the children stand in an orderly fashion in a semicircle. Give the first person on the left a striker and have him strike his bell. He passes the striker to the next child who strikes his bell and passes it on. You are looking for the highest or lowest note. We'll say it's the lowest. As the group listens and agrees on some notes which are among the lowest, have these children stand to one side. Those who are thus screened as possible lowest then each play again. The group decides which is lowest. The lowest stands at the extreme left of the line and strikes his bell. The searching, listening and grading continues until the process is complete. Then the children play each bell in turn. It should be the C scale.

Note: Collect strikers. Each child goes individually to replace his bell at the board.

5. Group tunes. Each child has one of the eight brown bells. They stand in the same order as the C scale from low to high. The teacher says, "Let's see if you can play when I point to you." After they are proficient, the teacher has them play a very simple tune, such as "Big Ben" or "Twinkle," by pointing to each child to play the desired note. Ask each child how many times he struck his note.

DIRECT AIM

To become conscious of how many times a note may be played in a tune. They also learn that not all the notes are always played.

6. Memory game. Assign a note to a number of children, saying, "John, this is your note. Would you like to see if you can recognize it later on?" Perhaps 30 minutes later, play the note and see if the child recognizes it.

LANGUAGE

After the child is proficient in pairing and grading, he can learn the names of the notes. Sing the names of three notes, C.E.G. Have the child sing them also. Sing them up and down. Teach by the three period lesson. If the child can read, place the labeled discs onto the base of the bells he knows. Control is always the white bells.

AGE

3 years onwards.
4 to 4½ years—ability to pair.
4½ to 5 years—ability to grade.

DIRECT AIMS

Discrimination of sounds.
Appreciation of music.
Discrimination of pitch.

Notation Boards

MATERIAL

Two green boards having five black lines plus a ledger line and four spaces.

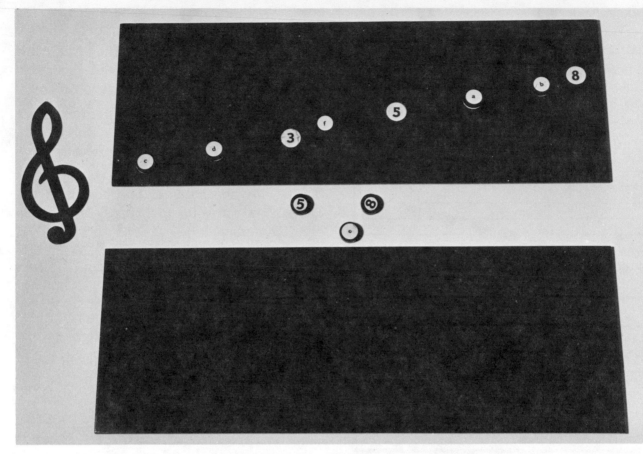

Fig. 60 — Notation Boards I and II With Movable Note Numbers and Names

Board 1 has the lines indented and eight cut-out circular spaces numbered to correspond to the places occupied by the notes.

There are also eight discs that can be fitted into the holes. Each disc has the name of the note written on one side and the number it bears in the scale on the reverse. The second board has no hollowed out spaces. There are 64 white discs bearing the note name only on the reverse side.

PRESENTATION

Board 1.

Teach the child which line or space the discs go on. C=1, D=2, E=3. The child matches the numbers to the correct position leaving the names uppermost. He then plays the notes. He checks to see if they are placed properly by simply turning the discs over. Then, after the child can place the discs easily, relate the bells to the stave board. Place bells opposite the notes on the board. Demonstrate with C.E.G. Play them. Allow child to continue.

PRESENTATION

Board 2.

Take discs at random, read the name and place it face downward on the stave. Do this until all discs are placed. Turn them over to see if correct.

EXERCISE 1

Sing notes or phrases and place discs accordingly.

EXERCISE 2

Using lightly drawn lines drawn on paper, children can compose tunes, play them on the bells and keep handy in a notebook. They can use the stave board first to work them out.

DIRECT AIM

To discover where the notes go in the stave.

INDIRECT AIM

To prepare for reading music.

Sight Reading Boards

Fig. 61 — Sight-Reading Boards

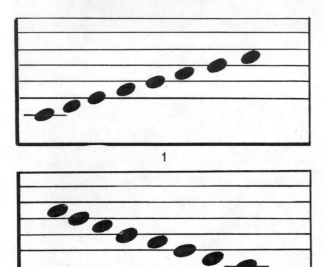

MATERIAL

A series of seventeen white boards upon which are painted the five black lines representing the stave. Each has a different pattern of notes, for example:

Board 1—C scale from middle C up one octave.

Board 2—The reverse of Board 1. C scale down to middle C.

Board 3—Pairs of alternating notes beginning with middle C, e.g., Cd, Ce, Cf, Cg, et cetera, up to C.

Board 4—The reverse of Board 3.

PRESENTATION

1. Boards 1 and 2 are presented before any others. Place in the room from time to time to stimulate or reflect interest (similar to classified cards).

2. With a group, hold the board up for all to see, then have them sing the notes. (This is *only* done after the child has worked with the stave and can recognize the notes.)

3. Have the group sing one of the note patterns, e.g., C scale upwards. Show them two boards and ask which notes they have sung.

4. Play the notes of one board on the bells. Ask someone to bring you the one you have played.

5. Give the child a note-board and ask him to play it on the bells.

6. Child records note patterns in his music book.

AIM

To make the child more aware of pitch. To introduce written music.

AGE

5½ to 6 years (approximately).

INTRODUCTION TO BASS CLEF

MATERIAL

Two stave boards which will fit together by means of sticks and corresponding holes. 64 white painted discs having the names of the scale on one side, also the letters.

PRESENTATION

Fasten the two boards together.

1. Make a rhombus using the white discs by placing them on the two stave boards. Begin with middle C and place a white disc for each note of ascending and descending C scale. Then say to the child, "Let's see what happens if we go below this board." Then place the white discs in descending order diagonally to lower C. Place the white discs in another diagonal line back up to middle C.

Fig. 62 — Notation Boards Joined to Introduce Bass Clef

2. Separate the two boards and compare the location of the notes. Lower C is the second space on the lower board, but the second space on the other board is A. Compare all the notes.

3. Introduce the clef signs.

Fig. 63 — Movable Clef, Sharp and Flat Signs

Treble or G Clef

Bass or F Clef

Sharp   Flat

Explain to the child that since the lines don't always mean the same thing, we have special signs to tell us where the notes are located.

Show him the movable g clef or treble clef sign and where it is placed. (The bull's eye goes around the g on the second line.)

Show him the movable f clef sign and where it is placed. The heavy dot is placed on the fourth line of the lower stave when it is f. Two dots are placed alongside each in a space above, or below the f, second line.

EXERCISE

Provide opportunity to practice with notes of the bass clef. He again makes the rhombus, removes the top half and uses it to place the white discs. Read the white disc, place it upside down on the stave. Select discs at random, and continue until all are placed. Turn them over and use the lower half of the rhombus as a control.

AIM

Introduce lower stave.

Introduce clef signs.

Preparation for writing and reading music.

91

6 years approximately.

LANGUAGE

G clef or treble clef.
F clef or bass clef.

MAJOR DIATONIC SCALE

MATERIALS

C scale brown bells. A box of cards marked "interval." A box of cards marked "tone" and "semitone."

Presentation

1. Arrange brown-based bells of C scale on the table, leaving a space where the black bells go.

2. Play the notes of the scale in sequence.

3. Next, play the first two notes together. Listen. Say, "There is an *interval* between those two notes. The second is higher than the first. Let's mark that interval with one of these cards." Place a card between the two bells C and D at the base. Do with D and E next and continue up the scale.

4. Point out the differences in the size of the intervals. Play two consecutive notes, such as D E, listen carefully. Play two other notes with a different interval, such as B C. Listen carefully. Then ask which two had the largest interval. "The first two notes are farthest apart. We call that interval a tone." Play it again. Play the second combination. "That interval is smaller. We call that a semitone." Play it again. Do this several times with all the combinations.

5. Introduce the cards saying tone and semitone. Play the scale pairing the notes as before. Place tone cards between whole intervals and semitone cards between bells having half-intervals.

6. Read the cards through and point out the pattern of tone, tone, tone, semitone, tone, tone, tone, semitone.

7. Give the language. All scales following this pattern are major diatonic scales.

EXERCISE 1

Give the child the cards and let him practice playing the notes and marking the tones and semitones.

EXERCISE 2

After he has practiced this material, tell him the scale is made up of two tetrachords (4 notes in each chord), dividing the scale into the upper four notes and lower four. Show that the lower four can be the beginning of another scale. Similarly, the upper four notes can be the lower half of another scale.

EXERCISE 3

Select any note as a starting point and apply the major diatonic pattern to build any major scale. Let the child practice.

AGE

6 years approximately.

AIMS

To make the child conscious of the intervals and the differences between them.

To introduce the tone pattern of major diatonic scales.

INTRODUCTION TO SHARPS AND FLATS

MATERIAL

Five brown-based bells corresponding to the black-based bells. Heretofore these have been kept separate from the other bells on the bell board.

Presentation 1

Ask the child if he'd like to find out what the separate brown bells sound like. Mix the brown bells. Strike one of the black bells. Listen. Find its mate from among the brown bells. Place it opposite the matching black bell on the board. Continue until all are matched and placed. Play all of the notes in sequence, beginning with middle C.

This is the chromatic scale. (The intervals are all semitones.) *Control*—black and white bells.

Presentation 2

Introduce the names of the black bells, then give the symbols. Select the first two notes of the C scale — C and D. Play them and tell the child they have their own names, C and D but the brown bell which goes between them doesn't really have a name of its own. When we talk about it, we have to refer to the names of the notes on either side. Show him by playing D. Then play the brown bell, which is lower. Explain that when we make something lower, we say we "flatten" it out. So the name of this note is D flat.

The same note can also be called C sharp, as it is making C a little higher. Do this with each of the sharps and flats (as the child is ready).

Presentation 3

Introduce the symbols for sharp and flat. Show him the movable symbols and tell him when the # sign is placed next to a note, it tells us to make that note sharp. The "b" sign means to flatten it.

EXERCISE

He can then practice writing these in his manuscript book and record the names of the chromatic scale and the symbols.

AGE

6 to 6½ years approximately.

AIM

To introduce the black bells. To make the child aware of sharps and flats.

HARMONIC MINOR SCALE

MATERIAL

The brown bells of the C major diatonic scale plus all of the black and white control bells on the bell board.

PRESENTATION

Tell the child you are going to show how to construct a different kind of a scale. (He already knows the C major diatonic pattern.)

1. Remove the C scale bells from the board and space them in order on the table in front of the bell board.

2. Play the scale. Listen.

3. Remove number 3 and substitute the black bell directly below. Put the brown bell back on the board. (Substitute E^b for E.)

4. Remove number 6 and substitute the black bell directly below it. Replace the number 6 bell on the board. (Substitute A^b for A.)

5. Play the new (harmonic minor) scale quite deliberately. Listen intently.

6. Tell the child, "We have just made the harmonic minor scale. Would you like to try it?" Together the directress and the child replace the bells on the board. The child then proceeds.

EXERCISES

1. The child can create tunes based upon this scale and record them in his music book.

2. The directress supplies the child with simple tunes based on the scale to read and play. He may also record these.

LANGUAGE

Tell the child the name of the scale is the harmonic minor scale. Explain that "minor" means smaller and refers to the fact that the intervals between notes 2 and 3 and also 5 and 6 are smaller than on the major diatonic. Play the first three notes of the *major* scale and then of the minor scale to demonstrate this clearly. Do the same thing with the 4th, 5th and 6th notes of each scale.

To construct the harmonic minor scale.
AGE
6 years onwards.

TONE BARS

MATERIAL

A series of twenty-five black and white wooden bars placed on a black and white painted board. The stripes of the board represent the piano keyboard.

The white stripes are in the pattern of a major diatonic scale. There are two complete octaves of tone bars, from middle C upwards. The tone is produced by striking a piece of metal set into the hollow wood bar with a wooden striker.

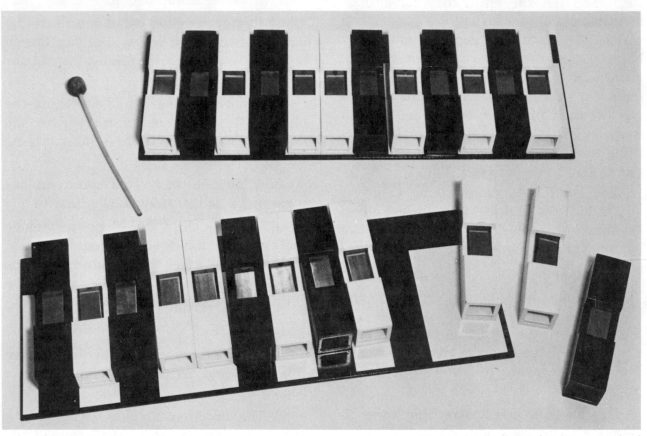

Fig. 64 — Tone Bars   —Photo taken at Eugene Montessori School

PRESENTATION

1. Ask the child if he would like to see how the tone bars work. Show him how to hold the striker and where to strike the bar. Let him do it.

2. Pull the tone bars resting on white spaces forward to meet the edge of the board. Play the scale. Ask the child if he recognizes it. He should be able to tell you it is the C major diatonic scale.

3. Tell the child he can pick any note he wishes—black or white—and you will build a major diatonic scale for him, starting with his note.

4. He chooses a starting point. Remove all tone bars to the left of that point and place in order behind the tone board.

5. Slide the remaining tone bars all the way down to the left.

6. Pull forward only those bars which are on the white stripes of the board.

7. Play the scale on these.

8. Ask the child if he'd like to try Stay with him until he understands the process.

EXERCISES

1. The child may build as many major diatonic scales as he wishes.

2. Play simple tunes based on these scales and record them.

LANGUAGE

Show the child how to find the names of the notes when he is ready. Count up from C to the starting point.

Use the letter names once only to any one scale. This rule determines whether you call a note a sharp or a flat.

ADDITIONAL LANGUAGE

To be introduced as the need arises:

1. Natural sign—this is used to negate a sharp or flat.

2. Key signature—this is written on the staffs and shows which notes are sharp or flat.

3. Bar lines (measure lines) — these mark the basic rhythm pattern. They are vertical lines placed on the staff immediately preceding the accent notes.

4. Time signature—two numerals, one placed directly above the other, are written on the staff at the beginning of a piece of music. They indicate the number of beats to a bar (or measure) and the kind of note used as a base.

MUSIC AND MOVEMENT

Music is first introduced to the child in nursery school as background or mood music for walking on the line. After the child is adept at walking on the line and has acquired good equilibrium, music then paves the way for moving in time to the rhythm played.

EXERCISES

Some suggested exercises follow. Many variations are possible.

Have the child practice walking or stepping in time to music, one step to each beat, two beats to a bar.

Change from two to three beats to a bar. See if the child notices and adjusts his walk.

Have the child clap to different rhythms. The directress claps and sees if the child, or group, can repeat the rhythm.

Later, have the children clap in time to music.

Have several children walk and clap to the music simultaneously.

Walk in time to the music but clap only on the accent notes.

Walking, running, skipping and marching rhythms are those to which a young child readily responds with his whole body. Once we have demonstrated a particular step, the child should be free to interpret the rhythms himself. The teaching of music cannot be too rigidly programmed. The teacher uses the techniques described over a long period of time, observing the child's progress and allowing him to explore at his own rate. Even without musical training the teacher can experiment and introduce many valid musical experiences to the young child.

Appendix

SOURCES OF MONTESSORI MATERIALS

*Montessori Leermiddelenhuis A. Nienhuis N.V.,
Industriepark 14,
Zelhem.-(Gelderland.)
The Netherlands

*Kaybee School Aids and Equipment Corporation
Factory C/3-C/4 Industrial Estate
Moula Ali-Hyderbad A.P.
India

A. Daigger and Co.
159 W. Kinzie Street
Chicago, Illinois 60610

Bibliography

Fisher, Dorothy Canfield. *Montessori for Parents*. Rev. ed. Cambridge, Massachusetts: Robert Bentley, Inc., 1965.

Fisher, Dorothy Canfield. *The Montessori Manual for Teachers and Parents*. Cambridge, Massachusetts: Robert Bentley, Inc., 1966.

Gitter, Lena. "The Montessori View of Art in Education." *Bulletin of Art Therapy*, Fall 1964.

Gitter, Lena. "A Picture Window to the World." *Academic Therapy*, Winter 1969.

Hainstock, Elizabeth. *Teaching Montessori in the Home*. New York: Random House, 1968

Montessori, Maria. *The Absorbent Mind*. Adyar, India: The Theosophical Publishing House, 1964.

Montessori, Maria. *The Advanced Montessori Method,* Vol. I. Adyar, India: Kalakshetra Publications, 1965.

Montessori, Maria. *The Child*. Adyar, India: The Theosophical Publishing House, 1965.

Montessori, Maria. *The Discovery of the Child*. Adyar, India: Kalakshetra Publications, 1962.

Montessori, Maria. *Dr. Montessori's Own Handbook*. New York: Schocken Books, 1965.

Montessori, Maria. "The Erdkinder and the Functions of the University Life." London, England: Maria Montessori Training Organization. [Booklet]

Montessori, Maria. *The Formation of Man*. Adyar, India: The Theosophical Publishing House, 1965.

Montessori, Maria. *The Secret of Childhood*. Calcutta, India: Orient Longmans, 1962.

Montessori, Maria. *To Educate the Human Potential*. Adyar, India: Kalakshetra Publications, 1948.

Salzman, Richard. "Montessori and the Revolution in Values." Keynote address, Montessori Centennial Celebration, Washington, D. C., 1970.

Standing, E. Mortimer. *Maria Montessori Her Life and Work*. New York: Mentor-Omega, 1962.

*Authorized by the Association Montessori Internationale, founded by Dr. Maria Montessori, to produce and distribute Montessori material.